NATIONAL 5

COMPUTING SCIENCE
2013 Specimen Question Paper
& 2013 Model Papers

HODDER
GIBSON
LEARN MORE

This book contains the official 2013 SQA Specimen Question Paper for National 5 Computing Science, with associated SQA approved answers modified from the official marking instructions that accompany the paper.

In addition the book contains model practice papers, together with answers, plus study skills advice. These papers, some of which may include a limited number of previously published SQA questions, have been specially commissioned by Hodder Gibson, and have been written by experienced senior teachers and examiners in line with the new National 5 syllabus and assessment outlines, Spring 2013. This is not SQA material but has been devised to provide further practice for National 5 examinations in 2014 and beyond.

Hodder Gibson is grateful to the copyright holders, as credited on the final page of the Answer Section, for permission to use their material. Every effort has been made to trace the copyright holders and to obtain their permission for the use of copyright material. Hodder Gibson will be happy to receive information allowing us to rectify any error or omission in future editions.

Hachette UK's policy is to use papers that are natural, renewable and recyclable products and made from wood grown in sustainable forests. The logging and manufacturing processes are expected to conform to the environmental regulations of the country of origin.

Orders: please contact Bookpoint Ltd, 130 Park Drive, Abingdon, Oxon OX14 4SE. Telephone: (44) 01235 827720. Fax: (44) 01235 400454. Lines are open 9.00–5.00, Monday to Saturday, with a 24-hour message answering service. Visit our website at www.hoddereducation.co.uk. Hodder Gibson can be contacted direct on: Tel: 0141 848 1609; Fax: 0141 889 6315; email: hoddergibson@hodder.co.uk

This collection first published in 2013 by
Hodder Gibson, an imprint of Hodder Education,
An Hachette UK Company
2a Christie Street
Paisley PA1 1NB

BrightRED Hodder Gibson is grateful to Bright Red Publishing Ltd for collaborative work in preparation of this book and all SQA Past Paper and National 5 Model Paper titles 2013.

Typeset by PDQ Digital Media Solutions Ltd, Bungay, Suffolk NR35 1BY

Printed in the UK

A catalogue record for this title is available from the British Library

ISBN: 978-1-4718-0203-4

3 2 1

2014 2013

Introduction

Study Skills – what you need to know to pass exams!

Pause for thought

Many students might skip quickly through a page like this. After all, we all know how to revise. Do you really though?

Think about this:

"IF YOU ALWAYS DO WHAT YOU ALWAYS DO, YOU WILL ALWAYS GET WHAT YOU HAVE ALWAYS GOT."

Do you like the grades you get? Do you want to do better? If you get full marks in your assessment, then that's great! Change nothing! This section is just to help you get that little bit better than you already are.

There are two main parts to the advice on offer here. The first part highlights fairly obvious things but which are also very important. The second part makes suggestions about revision that you might not have thought about but which WILL help you.

Part 1

DOH! It's so obvious but …

Start revising in good time

Don't leave it until the last minute – this will make you panic.

Make a revision timetable that sets out work time AND play time.

Sleep and eat!

Obvious really, and very helpful. Avoid arguments or stressful things too – even games that wind you up. You need to be fit, awake and focused!

Know your place!

Make sure you know exactly **WHEN and WHERE** your exams are.

Know your enemy!

Make sure you know what to expect in the exam.

How is the paper structured?

How much time is there for each question?

What types of question are involved?

Which topics seem to come up time and time again?

Which topics are your strongest and which are your weakest?

Are all topics compulsory or are there choices?

Learn by DOING!

There is no substitute for past papers and practice papers – they are simply essential! Tackling this collection of papers and answers is exactly the right thing to be doing as your exams approach.

Part 2

People learn in different ways. Some like low light, some bright. Some like early morning, some like evening / night. Some prefer warm, some prefer cold. But everyone uses their BRAIN and the brain works when it is active. Passive learning – sitting gazing at notes – is the most INEFFICIENT way to learn anything. Below you will find tips and ideas for making your revision more effective and maybe even more enjoyable. What follows gets your brain active, and active learning works!

Activity 1 – Stop and review

Step 1

When you have done no more than 5 minutes of revision reading STOP!

Step 2

Write a heading in your own words which sums up the topic you have been revising.

Step 3

Write a summary of what you have revised in no more than two sentences. Don't fool yourself by saying, 'I know it but I cannot put it into words'. That just means you don't know it well enough. If you cannot write your summary, revise that section again, knowing that you must write a summary at the end of it. Many of you will have notebooks full of blue/black ink writing. Many of the pages will not be especially attractive or memorable so try to liven them up a bit with colour as you are reviewing and rewriting. **This is a great memory aid, and memory is the most important thing.**

Activity 2 — Use technology!

Why should everything be written down? Have you thought about 'mental' maps, diagrams, cartoons and colour to help you learn? And rather than write down notes, why not record your revision material?

What about having a text message revision session with friends? Keep in touch with them to find out how and what they are revising and share ideas and questions.

Why not make a video diary where you tell the camera what you are doing, what you think you have learned and what you still have to do? No one has to see or hear it but the process of having to organise your thoughts in a formal way to explain something is a very important learning practice.

Be sure to make use of electronic files. You could begin to summarise your class notes. Your typing might be slow but it will get faster and the typed notes will be easier to read than the scribbles in your class notes. Try to add different fonts and colours to make your work stand out. You can easily Google relevant pictures, cartoons and diagrams which you can copy and paste to make your work more attractive and **MEMORABLE**.

Activity 3 – This is it. Do this and you will know lots!

Step 1

In this task you must be very honest with yourself! Find the SQA syllabus for your subject (www.sqa.org.uk). Look at how it is broken down into main topics called MANDATORY knowledge. That means stuff you MUST know.

Step 2

BEFORE you do ANY revision on this topic, write a list of everything that you already know about the subject. It might be quite a long list but you only need to write it once. It shows you all the information that is already in your long-term memory so you know what parts you do not need to revise!

Step 3

Pick a chapter or section from your book or revision notes. Choose a fairly large section or a whole chapter to get the most out of this activity.

With a buddy, use Skype, Facetime, Twitter or any other communication you have, to play the game "If this is the answer, what is the question?". For example, if you are revising Geography and the answer you provide is "meander", your buddy would have to make up a question like "What is the word that describes a feature of a river where it flows slowly and bends often from side to side?".

Make up 10 "answers" based on the content of the chapter or section you are using. Give this to your buddy to solve while you solve theirs.

Step 4

Construct a wordsearch of at least 10 X 10 squares. You can make it as big as you like but keep it realistic. Work together with a group of friends. Many apps allow you to make wordsearch puzzles online. The words and phrases can go in any direction and phrases can be split. Your puzzle must only contain facts linked to the topic you are revising. Your task is to find 10 bits of information to hide in your puzzle but you must not repeat information that you used in Step 3. DO NOT show where the words are. Fill up empty squares with random letters. Remember to keep a note of where your answers are hidden but do not show your friends. When you have a complete puzzle, exchange it with a friend to solve each other's puzzle.

Step 5

Now make up 10 questions (not "answers" this time) based on the same chapter used in the previous two tasks. Again, you must find NEW information that you have not yet used. Now it's getting hard to find that new information! Again, give your questions to a friend to answer.

Step 6

As you have been doing the puzzles, your brain has been actively searching for new information. Now write a NEW LIST that contains only the new information you have discovered when doing the puzzles. Your new list is the one to look at repeatedly for short bursts over the next few days. Try to remember more and more of it without looking at it. After a few days, you should be able to add words from your second list to your first list as you increase the information in your long-term memory.

FINALLY! Be inspired...

Make a list of different revision ideas and beside each one write **THINGS I HAVE** tried, **THINGS I WILL** try and **THINGS I MIGHT** try. Don't be scared of trying something new.

And remember – "FAIL TO PREPARE AND PREPARE TO FAIL!"

National 5 Computing Science

The National 5 Computing Science exam is worth 90 marks. That is 60% of your overall mark. The remaining 40% of your overall mark (60 marks) comes from the supervised assignment which you will complete in class.

The exam

Approximately half of the marks in the question paper will be awarded for questions related to *Software Design and Development*, and half to *Information Systems Design and Development*.

Candidates will complete the question paper in 1 hour and 30 minutes.

Section 1 will have 20 marks and will consist of short answer questions assessing breadth of knowledge from across both Units. Most questions will have 1–2 marks.

Section 2 will have 70 marks and will consist of approximately 6–8 extended response questions, each with approximately 8–12 marks. Questions will be of a problem-solving nature rather than direct recall and will include extended descriptions and explanations.

Questions related to Software Design and Development will cover the following areas:

- computational constructs and concepts
- explaining code
- writing code
- data types and structures
- software development — design, testing, documentation
- low level operations and computer architecture.

Questions related to programming will use the form of 'pseudocode' below:

Variable types: INTEGER, REAL, BOOLEAN, CHARACTER

Structured types: ARRAY, STRING

System entities: DISPLAY, KEYBOARD

Assignment: SET … TO …

Conditions: IF .. THEN .. (ELSE) … END IF

Conditional repetition: WHILE … DO … END WHILE

REPEAT … UNTIL …

Fixed repetition: REPEAT … TIMES … END REPEAT

Iteration: FOR .. FROM .. TO .. DO .. END FOR

FOR EACH … FROM … DO … END FOR EACH

Input/output: RECEIVE … FROM …

SEND … TO ..

Operations: -, +, *, /, ^, mod, &

Comparisons: =, [1], <, <=, >, >=

Logical operators: AND, OR, NOT

Pre-defined functions: id (parameters)

If you are required to write in code then you can use any programming language with which you are familiar.

Questions related to Information System Design and Development will cover the following areas:

- database design, structures, links and operations
- website design, structures and links
- coding (including HTML and Javascript)
- media types, including file size calculations
- information system development — purpose, features, user interface, testing
- technical implementation (hardware, software, storage, networking/connectivity)
- security, legal and environmental issues.

General advice

Remember to read the questions carefully and answer what is being asked.

Trade names

It is never acceptable to use a company name, such as Microsoft Access or Serif Web-Plus etc. in an answer. Use the generic terms such as databases, web-design packages.

Conversion

If you are asked to convert a number into an 8-bit binary number make sure that your answer has 8 bits!

Technical terminology

It is important that the correct technical terminology is used e.g. USB flash drive – not USB pen, USB stick, pen drive or other commonly used expressions.

Units

Remember, there are 1024 bytes in a Kilobyte, not 1000. There are:

- 1024 Kilobytes in a Megabyte
- 1024 Megabytes in a Gigabyte
- 1024 Gigabytes in a Terabyte.

Data structure

The only data structure you need to know at National 5 is one-dimensional arrays.

Memory

Many candidates confuse RAM memory with backing storage. Remember, RAM memory is used to store programs and data temporarily while the program is being used. Backing storage is used to hold programs and data permanently until you are ready to use them. When you open an application it is taken from the backing storage (e.g. hard disc drive) and placed into the RAM memory.

Technical implementation

Use your common sense when thinking about the reasons why you would choose a particular type of hardware. Does it have to be portable? Does it require fast processing ability? What is the most sensible storage device? What is the best networking solution for this particular task?

Calculating storage requirements

When calculating the storage requirements for photographs, too many candidates forget that DPI must be squared. Remember to multiply the number of bits required to store the colour – NOT the number of colours!

For example, an image measures 3 inches by 4 inches and has a resolution of 600dpi in 8 colours

= 3 x 4 x 600 x 600 x 3 (3 bits can give 8 combinations of colours)

= 12960000 bits = 12960000/8 =1620000 bytes

= 1620000/1024 = 1582.03 Kb = 1882.03 / 1024

= 1.54 Mb

Storage devices

Candidates often confuse the three main types of storage devices:

- Magnetic – hard disk drives, floppy disc drives, magnetic tape (DAT)

- Solid state – USB flash drives

- Optical – CD-ROM, CD-R, CD-RW, DVD-ROM, DVD-R, DVD-RW and Blu-Ray.

Computers and the Law

Candidates must give the correct full names of the appropriate laws such as the "Data Protection Act", "Computer Misuse Act", "Health & Safety Regulations", "Communications Act" and "Copyright, Design and Patents Act".

Interfaces

Many candidates forget why an interface is required. Remember that an interface changes electrical voltages, changes analogue to digital, buffers data and deals with control signals.

Pre-defined functions

Remember that pre-defined functions are built-in sections of code that have been written and tested and are available for programmers to use. They include common functions such as random numbers and rounding.

Good luck!

Remember that the rewards for passing National 5 Computing Science are well worth it! Your pass will help you get the future you want for yourself. In the exam, be confident in your own ability. If you're not sure how to answer a question, trust your instincts and just give it a go anyway. Keep calm and don't panic! GOOD LUCK!

N5

National
Qualifications
SPECIMEN ONLY

Mark

SQ08/N5/01

Computing Science

Date – N/A for specimen

Duration – 1 hour and 30 minutes

Fill in these boxes and read what is printed below.

Full name of centre

Town

Forename(s)

Surname

Number of seat

Date of birth

Day	Month	Year
D D	M M	Y Y

Scottish candidate number

Total marks — 90

SECTION 1 — 20 marks

Attempt ALL questions in this section.

SECTION 2 — 70 marks

Attempt ALL questions in this section.

Read all questions carefully before attempting.

Write your answers in the spaces provided, using **blue** or **black** ink.

Show all workings.

Before leaving the examination room you must give this booklet to the Invigilator.
If you do not, you may lose all the marks for this paper.

MARKS

SECTION 1 — 20 marks

Attempt ALL questions

1. Convert the value 25 into an 8-bit *binary* number. Show your working.　　1

> 128 64 32 16 8 4 2 units
> 0 0 0 1 1 0 0 1
> 16 + 8 + 1 = 24 + 1 = 25

2. Explain why the telephone number 07700 901012 should be stored as a *text field type* and not a *numeric field type*.　　1

> It has a "0" at the start, which would be dropped if stored as a numeric field type.

3. Name the *bus* used to transfer instructions from the main memory to the processor.　　1

> Data bus

4. Companies must adhere to *health and safety legislation* for employees using computer systems regularly.

   Adjustable workstation chairs allow computer users to change the height and seating position to prevent back ache.

   Name **one** other workstation feature and describe how it reduces a risk to health.　　1

> "Tilt and swivel" monitor. It can be moved to the correct angle in order to prevent eye strain or squinting.

5. Describe the purpose of *JavaScript scripting language*.　　2

> Used in order to add interactivity to HTML/web pages

6. Here is part of a database used to store information about cameras.

Brand	Model	Megapixels (mp)	Screen Size	Optical Zoom	Colour	Continuous Shooting (Fps)	Wide Angle	Price (£)
Yarxa	YX2300	16·6	3	21	Silver	14	21	£131.70
JK	JK1209	16	3	15	White	1·39		£95.99
Katichi	K1456AD	16	2·7	21	Red			£99.99
Gifipix	PH900	16	3	26	Black			£139.99
Yarxa	YX3500	14·1	3	21	Black	1	25	£129.99
Katichi	K2300WA	14	3	18	Black	1·2	28	£119.99
Gifipix	PH800	14	3	18	Black	1·2		£134.99
Katichi	K2800AD	14	2·7	26	Red			£139.99
Katichi	K2850AD	14	3	26	White			£142.99
Gifipix	PH500	14	3	24	Black	1·2	24	£147.99

Describe how the data has been sorted.   2

Megapixels (Descending), Price (Ascending)

MARKS

7. The *pseudocode* below shows how a program could store and process the race times (in seconds) of the finalists in a 100 m sprint.

```
Line 1. SET  alltimes  TO  [10.23, 10.1, 10.29, 9.9,
        10.12, 10.34, 9.99, 9.58]
Line 2. SET  fastest_time  TO  alltimes [0]
Line 3. FOREACH  time  FROM  alltimes  DO
Line 4.    IF  time  < fastest_time THEN
Line 5.         SET  fastest_time  TO  time
Line 6. END IF
Line 7. END FOREACH
Line 8. SEND ["The winner's time was: ", fastest_time]
        TO DISPLAY
```

State the most suitable *data structure* and *data type* for storing the highlighted variable (*alltimes*) used above.

2

Data type = Real

Data structure = 1D array

8. A *web page* can be found using the *URL*:

    http://www.thooons.co.uk/partymusic/party.html

    Identify the *file type* being accessed.

1

HTML

9. An online auction company has suffered a *Denial of Service attack*.

    (a) Describe what is meant by a *Denial of Service attack*.

1

Flooding a server with a large number of requests

    (b) Explain the effect it would have on *users*.

1

It would result in the server being unavailable to its intended users.

Total marks   2

MARKS | DO NOT WRITE IN THIS MARGIN

10. Describe **one** benefit of using *biometric sensors* for security.

1

Replace hard-to-remember passwords, which may be shared or observed.

11. Operating system design is developing to take account of smartphones and tablets. Describe **one** example of this.

1

Operating system must deal with input from a different range of input devices.

12. A college has just upgraded all the computer equipment used by staff.

Describe **one** issue that should be considered when disposing of the old equipment.

1

Ensure that all data is wiped from hard drives before disposal.

13. Describe the role of a *file server* in a *client server* network.

1

Provides central storage for all network users.

MARKS | DO NOT WRITE IN THIS MARGIN

14. Below is a section of code written in the programming language ALGOL.

```
begin
integer N;
Read Int(N);
begin
real array Data[1:N];
real sum, avg;
integer i;
sum:=0;
for i:=1 step 1 until N do
begin real val;
Read Real(val);
Data[i]:=if val<0 then -val else val
end;
for i:=1 step 1 until N do
sum:=sum   Data[i];
avg:=sum/N;
Print Real(avg)
end
end
```

State **two** techniques that the programmer could use to make this code more readable.

2

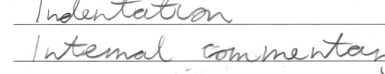
Indentation

Internal commentary

15. State **where** in a computer system the _binary_ instructions are stored before they are executed.

1

Memory

MARKS | DO NOT WRITE IN THIS MARGIN

SECTION 2 — 70 marks

Attempt ALL questions

16. An app is being developed for tourists to use to find out information about a holiday location such as: activities, how to get around, and the weather.

    When a tourist uses the app a number of options are displayed for their current location.

    (a) Describe **two** advantages of running this app on a smartphone rather than a desktop PC.　2

    ① Smartphones fit into pockets, and can easily be carried on holiday. ② Can access the internet anywhere, whereas a tablet may require wifi.

    (b) Comment on the suitability of the **user interface** design shown above for use on a smartphone.　2

    ① Straightforward navigation
    ② Good visual layout.

Question 16 (continued) | **MARKS** | DO NOT WRITE IN THIS MARGIN

(c) The temperature is displayed as 23·6 °C

State how this number would be stored by a computer system. **2**

Mantissa and exponent.

(d) The app will store photographs of the tourist attractions.

(i) State a *standard file format* suitable for storing photographs. **1**

Jpeg

(ii) The resolution of the photographs is reduced to make the file size smaller.

Explain why the file size of the photograph is reduced when the *resolution* is reduced. **1**

Because the image consists of less pixels.

Total marks 8

17. Road maps display the distance, in miles, between two points as a whole number.

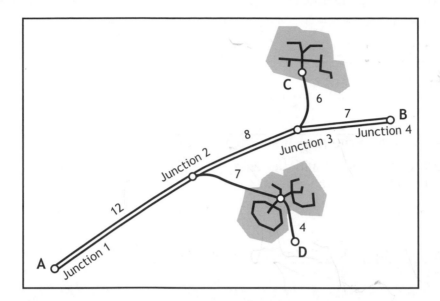

To calculate the total length of a journey between two places on the map, all sections of the journey are added together.

In the map shown, it is 23 miles (12+7+4) from A to D.

A program is designed to calculate the total length of a journey from a list of map distances. Journeys always start at A.

```
Line 1.    SET total TO 0
Line 2.    RECEIVE destination FROM keyboard
Line 3.    REPEAT
Line 4.        RECEIVE distance FROM keyboard
Line 5.        SET total TO total + distance
Line 6.    UNTIL distance = 0
Line 7.    SEND ["The distance between A and
           ",destination," is ",total," miles"] TO
           DISPLAY
```

(a) (i) The above design was created using *pseudocode*. Name another *design notation* that could have been used instead.   1

Structured diagram

(ii) Describe **one** advantage of using this *design notation* rather than *pseudocode*.   1

Gives a visual representation of the events in the program

Question 17 (continued)   MARKS

(b) Identify the *variables* and state their *data types* used in the program design.   3

Variable	Data type
1. destination	string
2. total	integer
3. distance	integer

(c) List the *test data* that should be entered to test that the program correctly calculates the distance from A to C.   2

distance = 12, 8, 6
0 to finish input

(d)
```
Line 1.  SET total TO 0
Line 2.  RECEIVE destination FROM keyboard
Line 3.  REPEAT
Line 4.        RECEIVE distance FROM keyboard
Line 5.        SET total TO total + distance
Line 6.  UNTIL distance = 0
```

The program above stops when the user enters 0.

The design is to be improved to display a warning message if the total is greater than 50.

Use pseudocode or a programming language of your choice to show how this extra feature could be implemented.   3

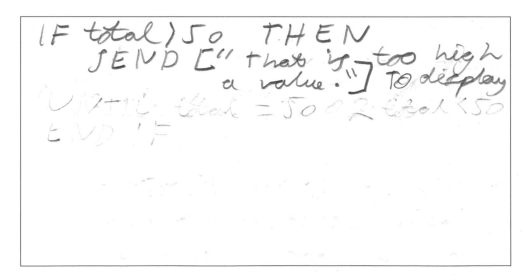

IF total > 50 THEN
  SEND ["that is too high a value."] TO display
UNTIL total = 50 or total < 50
END IF

Total marks 10

MARKS | DO NOT WRITE IN THIS MARGIN

18. The Lumecy Theatre homepage is shown below. It provides access to the four main sections of their website — What's On, Performers, Your Visit and Box Office. It also allows customers to go to the website of their sponsor.

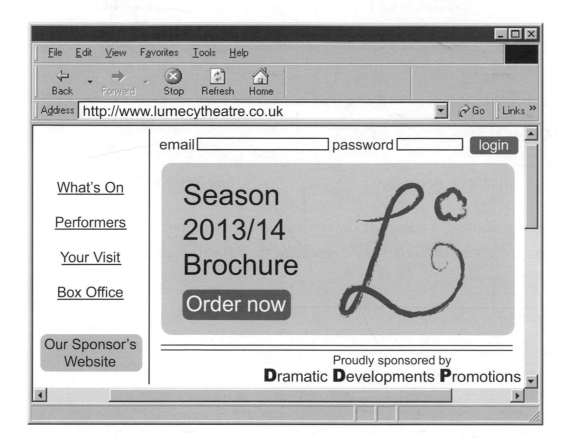

(a) The *hyperlinks* are checked to make sure each one leads to the correct **web page**.

Describe **one** other test that should have taken place when this **web page** was being developed.   1

Check "Order now" button: ensure that script executes correctly, and links to correct entry form

(b) Explain, using examples from the web pages above, the difference between an *internal hyperlink* and an *external hyperlink*.   2

"What's On" is an internal hyperlink. It takes the user to another web page on the same website. "Our Sponsor's Website" is an external hyperlink: it takes the user to a completely different website.

Question 18 (continued)

MARKS

Here are two sample pages from the Lumecy Theatre website.

What's On web page

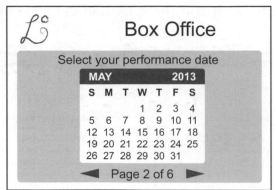

Box Office web page

(c) The two web pages above use different types of navigation.

Draw a diagram for each page to represent the navigation structure used.   **2**

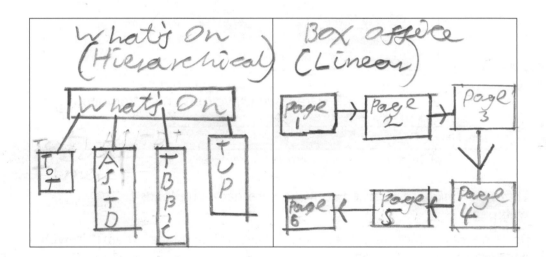

(d) Describe **one** element of good design that could be used to aid *accessibility* in the Lumecy website.   **1**

Careful choice of font helps readability

Question 18 (continued)

(e) Lumecy stores details of its customers on a database.

   (i) State **one** principle Lumecy must comply with in terms of the **Data Protection Act.**

1

Personal data must not be kept any longer than necessary

   (ii) Explain why compliance with this principle is important to **customers.**

1

Customers know that their data will be destroyed after a certain period of time

Total marks   8

19. Modern cars are fitted with embedded (built-in) computers that perform a variety of functions. One of the latest functions automatically activates the brakes if the car gets too close to the car in front. For safety reasons this function is only activated at low speeds.

   (a) Automatic braking requires sensors that measure the speed of the car and the distance between the two cars.

   State the hardware that allows external devices to be connected to a computer system.

1

Interfaces

Question 19 (continued)

(b) A program is required that will apply the car brakes if the distance between the two cars is less than 15 metres (m). For safety reasons, the brakes should only be activated if the speed of the car is less than 30 mph. The brakes should be kept on until the speed of the car is 0 mph.

23 mph

13·7 m

The *pseudocode* below shows a design for the program.

There are two errors in the logic of the program design. Find and describe each error made.

2

```
Line 1.    RECEIVE speed_of_car FROM (real) SENSOR
Line 2.    RECEIVE distance_to_car FROM (real) SENSOR
Line 3.    IF speed_of_car <30 OR distance_to_car<15 THEN
Line 4.    REPEAT
Line 5.        SEND apply brakes TO car brakes
Line 6.        RECEIVE speed_of_car FROM (real) SENSOR
Line 7.    UNTIL speed_of_car = 100
Line 8.    END IF
```

Error	Line number	Description
1.	3	OR should be AND
2.	7	100 should be 0

Question 19 (continued)   MARKS | DO NOT WRITE IN THIS MARGIN

(c) A program is written and tested using the following *test data*.

(i) Complete the table below to show four examples of *test data* and the type of each example.   3

Test data	Type of test data
car speed — 30 mph, distance — 15 m	*extreme*
car speed — 14 mph, distance — 8 m	normal
car speed — 45 mph, distance — 17 m	*extreme*
car speed — 100mph, d — 1000m	exceptional

(ii) Explain the purpose of fully testing a program using a variety of *test data*.   1

In order to ensure that the program can cope with a variety of inputs without crashing

Total marks   7

20. Carlton Crafts employs a number of instructors to run courses for clients. Here is an example of the data stored about each instructor and the courses they run.

Instructor ID	First Name	Surname	Date of birth	Expertise	Photo	Course ref	Title	Level	Course day
INS186	Oliver	Jones	12/11/85	Painting		DR234	Basic Drawing	Beginner	Monday
INS187	Susan	Kyama	25/11/87	Enamel		CR657	Jewellery Gifts	Advanced	Tuesday
INS186	Oliver	Jones	12/11/85	Painting		DR254	Painting Landscapes	All levels	Wednesday
INS188	Andrew	Cheng	09/09/90	Pottery		PY675	Drawing	Beginner	Tuesday

A decision is made to store this data in a database.

MARKS

(a) Describe one reason why a database with *linked tables* would be better than a *flat file* for storing this data.   1

No data duplication - Instructor details would only appear once

(b) A design with two tables is created—INSTRUCTOR table and COURSE table.

  (i) Identify a suitable *primary key* for each table.   2

INSTRUCTOR - Instructor ID
COURSE - Course ref.

  (ii) Explain why it is necessary to have a *foreign key*.   1

In order to link the tables. The foreign key is the primary key in the other table.

Question 20 (continued)

MARKS

DO NOT
WRITE IN
THIS
MARGIN

(c) Name **two** different *field types* required to store the data shown.   2

① Text

② Date

(d) Name and describe a type of *validation* that could be used on the field called "Course day".   2

Restricted choice: the user chooses from a list of acceptable values (the days of the week)

The following e-mail is received by one of the instructors who is a registered customer of YourMoni Bank Plc.

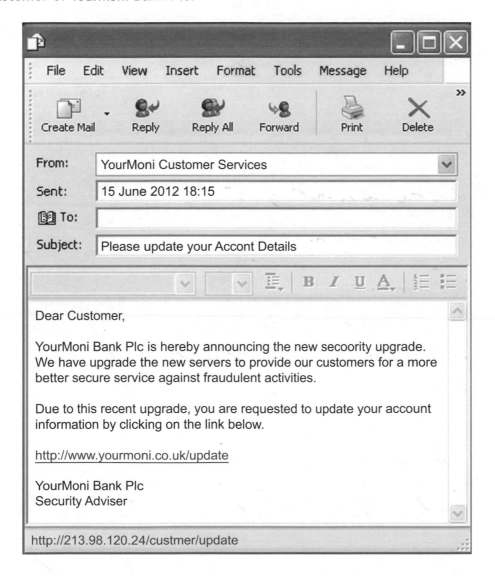

File   Edit   View   Insert   Format   Tools   Message   Help

Create Mail   Reply   Reply All   Forward   Print   Delete

From: YourMoni Customer Services

Sent: 15 June 2012 18:15

To:

Subject: Please update your Accont Details

B *I* U A

Dear Customer,

YourMoni Bank Plc is hereby announcing the new secoority upgrade. We have upgrade the new servers to provide our customers for a more better secure service against fraudulent activities.

Due to this recent upgrade, you are requested to update your account information by clicking on the link below.

http://www.yourmoni.co.uk/update

YourMoni Bank Plc
Security Adviser

http://213.98.120.24/custmer/update

Question 20 (continued)   MARKS

(e) Explain why the instructor might suspect this is not a genuine e-mail from the bank. Your explanation should refer to **two** features of the email which could cause suspicion.   2

① Spelling mistakes. Unusual for a professional company.
② "Dear customer" instead of using his/her name.

(f) Explain why such e-mails pose a security risk if the recipient clicks on the link.   2

① Hackers may be attempting to steal personal details in order to access bank accounts.

Total marks 12

② Hacking of online details may lead to online fraud or identity theft

MARKS | DO NOT WRITE IN THIS MARGIN

21. A programming language provides the following built-in functions.

move(n)   n = distance moved in pixels

turn(d)   d = degrees turned (positive means clockwise)

pen_down()   starts drawing line

pen_up()   finishes drawing line

These can be used by the programmer to draw lines.

An example program, its output and notes on the output are shown below.

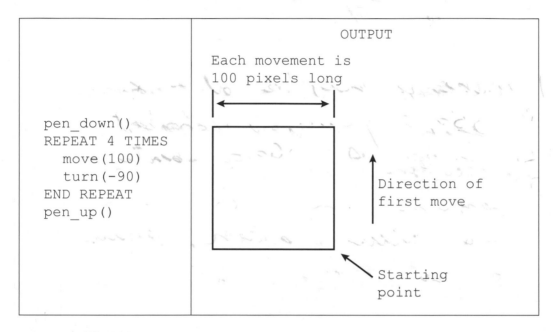

```
OUTPUT

Each movement is
100 pixels long
```

```
pen_down()
REPEAT 4 TIMES
   move(100)
   turn(-90)
END REPEAT
pen_up()
```

Direction of first move

Starting point

(a) Assuming the initial move direction is up the screen, draw the output that would be created by the following program.   **3**

```
pen_down()
REPEAT 2 TIMES
   move(30)
   turn(90)
   move(60)
   turn(-90)
END REPEAT
pen_up()
```

Question 21 (continued)

MARKS

DO NOT WRITE IN THIS MARGIN

(b) State the **type** of loop shown in the design. Justify your answer.

2

Fixed loop: it is repeated a fixed number of times

(c) Once the program has produced a drawing on screen, the user can save a drawing as a bitmap with a resolution of 600x600 pixels in 8 bit colour.

Calculate the *storage requirements* of one of these saved *bitmapped graphics*. Give your answer in appropriate units.

Show your working.

3

$$600 \times 600 = 360,000 \text{ pixels}$$
$$\text{Number of bits/pixel} = 8$$
$$8 \times 360,000 = 2,880,000 \text{ bits}$$
$$2,880,000 / 8 = 360,000 \text{ bytes}$$
$$360,000 / 1024 = 351.6 KB$$

Total marks   8

MARKS | DO NOT WRITE IN THIS MARGIN

22. The "Files in the Sky" website provides internet-based document storage. Before using the website, a user must set up a new account. The design for the new account input screen is shown below.

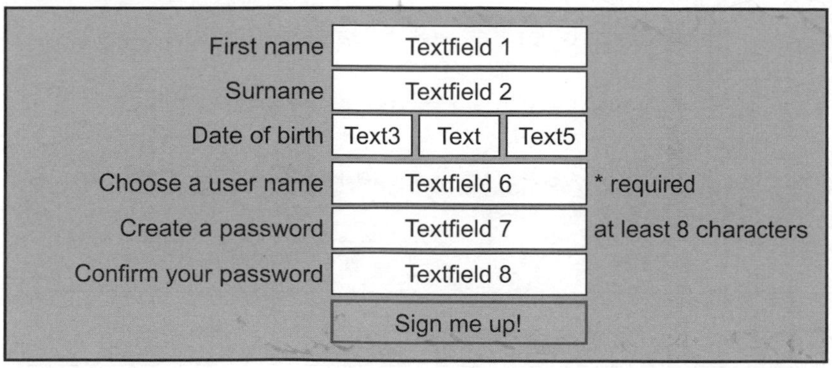

First name	Textfield 1
Surname	Textfield 2
Date of birth	Text3 Text Text5
Choose a user name	Textfield 6 * required
Create a password	Textfield 7 at least 8 characters
Confirm your password	Textfield 8
	Sign me up!

(a) (i) Using pseudocode or a language of your choice, show how a program could check that the password entered into textfield7 has at least eight characters.

3

REPEAT

IF textfield7) = 8 THEN
    SET valid to true
END IF

Question 22 (a) (continued)

(ii) Describe clearly, with reference to values and variables, what the following *pseudocode* does.

3

```
Line 1    SET password_entered TO textfield7
Line 2    SET password_confirm TO textfield8
Line 3    IF password_entered = password_confirm
          THEN
Line 4        proceed to newuserscreen
Line 5    ELSE
Line 6        SEND ["error occurred"] TO DISPLAY
Line 7    END IF
```

Values entered on form for "Create a password" and "Confirm your password" assigned to variables. If statement used in order to confirm these variables. If the values match, then a screen is shown confirming registration. Otherwise, an error message is displayed.

(b) Describe **two** advantages to a user deciding to use the "Files in the Sky" website rather than a USB flash drive to store documents.

2

① Cloud storage is scalable to requirements, whereas USB flash drives have a fixed capacity.

Total marks   8

② Cloud storage is less vulnerable to loss, damage or theft than a USB flash drive.

MARKS | DO NOT WRITE IN THIS MARGIN

23. A computer program is used to store a patient's heart rate each day for a week. The seven readings are stored in an array of real numbers called "bpm".

(a) Using pseudocode or a programming language of your choice, write a short program to calculate the average heart rate of the patient over the seven days.   3

> For days 1-7
>   let total = total + bpm (days)
> next days
>   let average = total / 7

(b) The pseudocode below shows how the heart rate is entered.

```
Line 1    REPEAT
Line 2        RECEIVE bpm FROM keyboard
Line 3        IF bpm < 35 THEN
Line 4            SEND appropriate message TO display
Line 5        END IF
Line 6    UNTIL bpm >=35
```

Describe all the events that will occur if a user enters a negative value.   3

> Line 6: conditions in cond: loop not met, since number entered is negative. Line 3: Input new value from keyboard. Line 3: The if condition, in the if statement, is met, since the no. is negative. An error message is displayed, and the user is asked to re-enter.

Question 23 (continued) **MARKS** DO NOT WRITE IN THIS MARGIN

(c) The completed program is translated into *binary* using a compiler.

(i) State the name given to binary instructions. **1**

Machine code

(ii) State **two** reasons why a *compiler* is used to translate the completed program. **2**

(1) Can create portable code

(2) Code will execute more quickly.

Total Marks 9

[END OF SPECIMEN QUESTION PAPER]

NATIONAL 5

2013 Model Paper 1

HODDER
GIBSON
LEARN MORE

National Qualifications
MODEL PAPER 1

Computing Science

Duration — 1 hour and 30 minutes

Total marks — 90

SECTION 1 — 20 marks

Attempt ALL questions in this section.

SECTION 2 — 70 marks

Attempt ALL questions in this section.

Read all questions carefully before attempting.

Write your answers in the spaces provided, using **blue** or **black** ink.

Show all workings.

MARKS | DO NOT WRITE IN THIS MARGIN

SECTION 1 — 20 marks

Attempt ALL questions

1. State how a computer system represents characters.   1

    Binary

2. Convert the *binary* number 100001 into a *decimal* number. Show all working.   1

    128 64 32 16   8   4   2   1
    0   0   1   0   0   0   0   1

    32 + 1 = 33

3. Explain how data is transferred from the *memory* into the *processor*.   1

    Buses

4. Dot has received a text file from her friend Sara but is unable to access it with her text processing software. Explain how you can ensure that another computer user can access your text processing files that you have sent them.   1

    Save them as a standard file formats, such as RTF.

5. Solid state storage devices are much more difficult to damage than magnetic disks. State **two** reasons why some laptop manufacturers are still using magnetic disks.   2

    Not as expensive and not such a high storage capacity

6. Explain the advantage of using *cloud storage* compared to local servers.   1

    Can be accessed from anywhere in the world.

7. Describe what should happen to the data when you are accessing on-line banking?   1

    It should be encrypted.

MARKS

8. State the *law* you are breaking when you download a film from the Internet without paying for it.

1

Copyright, Designs and Patents Act.

9. Name a *standard design notation* that you could use to plan a solution to a problem.

1

Structured diagram

10. Describe why *keylogging* is such a security risk.

2

The first thing that you type are your username and password, which would be accessible to the person doing the keylogging the software

11. Marion is looking at two laptops in a shop but is unsure which she should buy. State **two** criteria, which would help you decide which laptop was better than another.

2

RAM size, processor speed

12. The *pseudocode* below shows a selection of code to decide whether you are entitled to a school bus pass.

```
Line 1. IF age>5 OR age<18 THEN
Line 2. SEND ["Eligible for School Bus Pass"] TO DISPLAY
Line 3. END IF
```

When tested the program is found to have an error.

Explain the error in the program.

1

OR should be AND

13. Explain why the following code is not good practice.

1

```
Line 1.      RECEIVE L FROM keyboard
Line 2.      RECEIVE b FROM keyboard
Line 3.      SET A TO L*B
Line 4.      SEND[A] TO DISPLAY
```

No meaningful identifiers

MARKS DO NOT WRITE IN THIS MARGIN

14. State the task you would be undertaking if you were using *HTML*? **1**

Web creation

15. Explain what a *hyperlink* is used for in a web page. **1**

Moving to another webpage

16. State the type of *construct* used in the following code. **1**

```
Line 1.     REPEAT
Line 2.                 RECEIVE code FROM KEYBOARD
Line 3.     UNTIL code=7741
Line 4.     DISPLAY ["Door Open"]
```

Conditional loop

17. State the type of *error* you have if you make a spelling mistake when typing in your code. **1**

Syntax error

MARKS | DO NOT WRITE IN THIS MARGIN

SECTION 2 – 70 marks

Attempt ALL questions

MARKS

18. Michelle has to buy 20 computers to replace the old stand-alone Desktop computers that her company use at present.

    (a) Describe **two** advantages of replacing the Desktop computers with tablet computers.   2

    ① Portable

    ② Small carbon footprint

    (b) Michelle's friend suggests that she should link the new computers using a *peer to peer network* rather than a *client server network* as it's cheaper.

    Describe **two** reasons why this is not a good solution.   2

    ① No security
    ② Difficult to create a
       methodical backup
       regime.

    (c) Michelle wants the new computers to use *Biometric security*.

    Describe **two** different ways in which computers can use Biometric security.   2

    ① Retina scanning: confirming
       ID by scanning eye retinas
    ② Fingerprints. They are
       unique to a person, and can
       be recognised by fingerprint scanners

    (d) Describe what *data security precaution* the company must undertake with the old computers before they are de-commissioned.   1

    Ensure that all data is wiped
    from hard drives. Physical
    destruction of hard discs
    if data cannot be
    removed by software.

Question 18 (continued)

MARKS

(e) Describe what should happen to the old equipment now that the company no longer want it.

2

Ensure that the equipment is recycled or re-used. The metals inside should be safely extracted.

Total marks   9

19. A program is required to display a motorway warning sign if a truck is:

- higher than 200cm

- heavier than 2.4 tonnes

```
Line 1      RECEIVE weight FROM sensor
Line 2      RECEIVE height  FROM sensor
Line 3      IF                                    THEN
Line 4              DISPLAY["Do not proceed"]
Line 5              DISPLAY["Turn left at next junction"]
Line 6      END IF
```

(a) Complete the missing *pseudocode* for line 3.   3

IF weight > 200 OR weight > 2·4 THEN
THEN

(b) Complete the table below to show what *test data* you would use to test the program.   3

Type of test data	Test Data	
Normal	Height - 150cm, weight -	2 tonnes
Extreme	Height - 201cm, weight -	2·5 tonnes
Exceptional	Height - 500cm, weight -	3 tonnes

Question 19 (continued)   **MARKS**

(c) Describe what should happen if you test the program with *negative data*.   **1**

As it should be impossible to have a height or weight less than 0, the program should ask for a + value.

(d) The information from the sensors is sent to the local Police CCTV operators who check that the trucks turn left at the next junction.

State the most appropriate method of transmitting the *data* from the sensor to the Police computer.   **1**

A wireless connection.

Total marks   8

20. A programming language provides the following pre-defined functions.

```
Right(d) - turns right d number of degrees

Left(d) - turns left d number of degrees

Forward(p) - Draws a line of p pixels

Move(p) - moves without drawing a line of p pixels
```

E.g. To draw a triangle our code would be

Pseudocode	Output

Right(30)
 Forward(100)
 REPEAT 2 TIMES
      Right(120)
      Forward(100)
 END REPEAT	

Question 20 (continued)

MARKS | DO NOT WRITE IN THIS MARGIN

(a) Write the *code* that would create the following output: **3**

Pseudocode	Output

REPEAT 4 TIMES
  Forward (100)
  Right (90)
ENDREPEAT
Right (135)
Move (50)
Left (135)
REPEAT 4 TIMES
  Forward (100)
  Right (90)
END REPEAT	

(b) The graphic could be saved as a *bit-mapped graphic* or a *vector graphic*.

Describe **two** advantages of saving the graphic as a vector compared to a bit-mapped.   **2**

① Less memory required

② Not resolution dependant

(c) The graphic is saved as a bit-map image with a resolution of 400 x 400 pixels using four colours.

Calculate the storage requirements of the graphic. Give your answer in appropriate units.

Show your working.   **3**

400 x 400 x 2 = 320,000 bits

320,000 / 8 = 40,000 bytes

40,000 / 1024 = 39.1 KB

(d) Name a *standard file format* that you may use to save the graphic.   **1**

Bmp / Jpeg

Total marks **9**

MARKS

21. Bright Red Publishing have multiple choice tests available on the Internet like the example below.

How many bytes are in a Kilobyte?	
A	8
B	1000
C	1024
D	8192

The user types in the letter that corresponds to the correct answer.

(a) Describe **two** problems that this type of Interface could have.   2

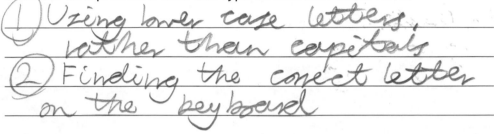

1) Using lower case letters, rather than capitals

2) Finding the correct letter on the keyboard

(b) Using pseudocode or a language of your choice, write the *Input Validation psuedocode* which will validate that the input is either A, B, C or D.   4

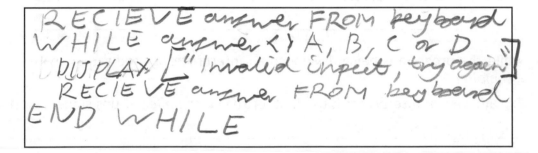

```
RECIEVE answer FROM keyboard
WHILE answer <> A, B, C or D
  DISPLAY ["Invalid input, try again"]
  RECIEVE answer FROM keyboard
END WHILE
```

Question 21 (continued)

MARKS | DO NOT WRITE IN THIS MARGIN

(c) Describe clearly with reference to *values* and *variables*, what the following *pseudocode* does.   **3**

```
Line 1.      SET wrong=0
Line 2.      SET right=0
Line 3.      RECEIVE answer FROM keyboard
Line 4.      IF answer=C THEN
Line 5.          SET correct=correct+1
Line 6.      ELSE
Line 7.          SET wrong=wrong +1
Line 8.      END IF
```

Initiates the variables "right" and "wrong" 5 the value of 0. If answer from keyboard = C, then +1 to the "correct" variable; otherwise, +1 to the "wrong" variable.

(d) While the program is being developed an *interpreter* is used rather than a *compiler*.

Explain why an *interpreter* is used rather than a *compiler* at this stage.   **1**

Thong errors

Total marks 10

MARKS | DO NOT WRITE IN THIS MARGIN

22. Heatcon make Central Heating controllers that turn on the heating when it becomes cold and turn them off when it becomes too warm.

   (a) The *pseudocode* below shows how the heating is controlled.

   ```
   Line 1          REPEAT
   Line 2          RECIEVE temperature FROM sensor
   Line 3          IF temperature<10 THEN
   Line 4                SEND on TO boiler
   Line 5          END IF
   Line 6          IF temperature>20 THEN
   Line 7                SEND off TO boiler
   Line 8          END IF
   Line 9          UNTIL switch = off
   ```

   Describe all the events that will occur when you run the program if the sensor gives a temperature of **16.3 degrees.**   4

   Line 2 - Value of temperature (16·3°) is entered

   Line 3 - Checks if temperature is less than 10 - No, so it goes to line 5.

   Line 6 - Checks if temperature is greater than 20 - No, so it goes to line 8.

   Line 9 - Goes back to line 1, unless switch

   (b) Explain how the value for temperature is stored in the computer system.   2

   Mantissa and exponent

Question 22 (continued)

MARKS

DO NOT
WRITE IN
THIS
MARGIN

(c) State the *data type* that is used for the variable boiler in this program.

Boolean

1

(d) Explain what connects the computer systems to the actual boiler and sensors to allow them to be controlled.

Interfaces

1

(e) Describe what the programmer should have put in the program to help with future maintenance.

Internal commentary

1

Total marks   9

23. "MegaToten" are a rock band who are going to keep a database of their fans to keep them informed of their concerts and new releases.

ID	Name	Address	Town	E-Mail Address	New CD
0001	John Smith	7 Dundee Street	Dundee	john.smith854@Hmail.co.uk	Yes
0002	Aleesha Khan	15 Mountcastle Drive	Edinburgh	AleeshaAOK@Coldmail.com	No
0003	Ian Brown	112 Fairfield Cres	Glasgow	Ibrown@Coldmail.com	No
0004	Peter Gabriel	65 Lorne Ave	Glasgow	peteGabriel77@Hmail.co.uk	No
0005	Dmitri Simpson	17 Earls Drive	Dundee	Dsimpson@dead.co.uk	Yes
0006	Sergei Simpson	17 Earls Drive	Dundee	Ssimpson@dead.co.uk	Yes
0007	Alison Krauss	119 Broadfoot Mains	Glasgow	AlisonK@Hmail.co.uk	No
0008	Pablo Hewitt	82 Sea View	Elgin	Phewitt@coldmail.com	No
0009	Karen Brown	5 Parkhead View	Newcastle	Kbrown@unique.com	Yes
0010	Bridget Hunter	11 Traquair Park East	Montrose	BBHunter@Coldmail.com	No

(a) State the most appropriate field type for the "New CD" field.

Boolean

1

(b) State the most appropriate field type for the "E-Mail" field.

Text

1

Question 23 (continued)

MARKS

DO NOT WRITE IN THIS MARGIN

(c) The ID field is a *primary key*. Explain the purpose of a *primary key* in a database.

1

To uniquely identify each individual record.

(d) Explain what "MegaToten" should do before storing any personal data.

1

Register with the Office of the Information Comissioner

(e) Explain how you would find all the fans who had bought a CD in Dundee.

3

Search on the field "New CD" = yes, AND on the town field = "Dundee"

(f) State **one** limitation of storing data in a flat file database.

1

Data duplication

Question 23 (continued)

MARKS | DO NOT WRITE IN THIS MARGIN

(g) State the type of *verification* that could be used on the field called Address.   1

None: an address could be any combination of text.

Total marks   9

24. "CoolDesigns" have designed a website for the ScotX clothing company.

Here is the design of their proposed web-site.

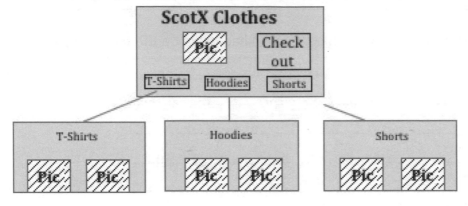

(a) State the error that "CoolDesigns" have made in the *navigation design* of the website.   1

No return to home page buttons on the web pages

(b) State the type of *navigation* that the website will use.   1

Hyperlinks

(c) Describe **two** tests that you would undertake on the completed website.   2

Links work
Checkout works

(d) Suggest an appropriate URL for the website.   2

www.SCOTXCLOTHES-co.uk

Question 24 (continued)   MARKS

(e) State a development in *security software* which has given confidence to customers in online purchasing.   1

Encryption

(f) State how "ScotX" can make sure that their website is near the top of any lists produced by search engines.   1

Use appropriate tags.

(g) Code was added that allowed the graphic to be *animated* when the pointer moves over it.

State the feature of *web-authoring software* that allows code to be added to the site.   1

Scripting language

Total marks   9

25. This program has been designed to get each day of the week's rainfall in millimetres and give an average week's rainfall.

```
Line 1    SET Total TO 0
Line 2    FOR loop FROM 1 TO 7 DO
Line 3            RECEIVE day FROM keyboard
Line 4            RECEIVE rainfall FROM keyboard
Line 5            SET total TO total + rainfall
Line 6    END LOOP
Line 7    SET average TO average/7
Line 8    SEND ["The average weekly rainfall is ",
          average] TO DISPLAY
```

(a) Explain why Total is initialised to 0 at the beginning of the program.   1

In case it has previously been used as a variable, and already contains a value

MARKS | DO NOT WRITE IN THIS MARGIN

Question 25 (continued)

(b) State the type of *loop* being used in this program.   1

Fixed loop

(c) State the type of *expression* being used in line 7.   1

Arithmetic expression

(d) State the data types of the following variables   3

Variable	Data type
Total	*Integer*
Day	*String*
Average	*Real*

(e) State what *data structure* would be required if you wanted to keep the values of the rainfall for each day.   1

1 Dimensional array

Total marks   7

[END OF PRACTICE QUESTION PAPER]

2013 Model Paper 2

National
Qualifications
MODEL PAPER 2

Computing Science

Duration — 1 hour and 30 minutes

Total marks — 90

SECTION 1 — 20 marks

Attempt ALL questions in this section.

SECTION 2 — 70 marks

Attempt ALL questions in this section.

Read all questions carefully before attempting.

Write your answers in the spaces provided, using **blue** or **black** ink.

Show all workings.

HODDER
GIBSON
LEARN MORE

MARKS | DO NOT WRITE IN THIS MARGIN

SECTION 1 — 20 marks

Attempt ALL questions

1. When you download music from the Internet it is in *MP3* format. Explain why some people prefer the *WAV* format that you find on a Compact Disc. **1**

   MP3 has had some data removed, while WAV has had no data removed.

2. What type of *error* occurs in a program when you make a spelling mistake in the code? **1**

   Syntax error.

3. Explain how the number 37.4 is stored in a computer system. **2**

   Mantissa and exponent.

4. A section of HTML code is shown below.

   <b>The Kitchen Stools<u>New Album</u>

   Explain why it does not show the correct *formatting* when the code is run. **1**

   The bold tag has not been closed.

5. State which *bus* pinpoints the correct memory location in memory where data is to be saved? **1**

   Address bus

6. State the purpose of a *string variable* in a computer program. **1**

   To store text

7. Explain why a *translator* is needed for programs written in a high level language. **1**

   In order to convert a high level language into machine code, so that it can be understood by the computer

8. Describe what you could change to allow you to store more photographs on your digital camera without increasing the capacity of the memory card. **1**

   Decrease resolution

MARKS | DO NOT WRITE IN THIS MARGIN

9. Mia has discovered that her next-door neighbour has been accessing her wireless network.

   (a) State which *law* her neighbours have broken.   1

   Communications Act, C. Misuse Act

   (b) Describe how Mia can prevent her neighbours accessing her wireless network.   1

   Passwords

10. State an advantage that a peer-to-peer network has over a client-server network.   1

    No additional hardware or software required. File server not required

11. Here is part of a database used to store information on a group of family and friends.

Forename	Surname	Address	Town	Date of Birth
Sally	Thompson	44 Dundas Street	Edinburgh	04/05/1961
Kausar	Ali	22 Sighthill Terrace	Glasgow	22/04/1992
Denise	Shivas	70 Queens Ave	Perth	12/01/1999
Ashima	Khan	11 George Street	Inverness	06/01/1975
Clair	Kerr	38 Broomhall Avenue	Kinross	28/03/1988
Joan	Sutherland	55 St. Johns Drive	Glasgow	28/02/1992
Iain	McKenzie	17 Home Street	Edinburgh	03/07/1995
Martin	Dailly	24 Castle Street	Inverness	14/09/2001
Michael	Ure	82 Echline Drive	Kirkcaldy	24/08/1956
Susan	Lamb	14 Dundee Street	Montrose	09/09/2001
Graham	Jackson	120 Hamilton View	Glasgow	04/11/1992
Paula	Hart	17 Glasgow Road	Edinburgh	16/03/1984

Describe what process would result in the solution being Martin Dailly.   3

Search on the "town" field = Inverness, AND "Date of birth" <1996

MARKS | DO NOT WRITE IN THIS MARGIN

12. The *pseudocode* below shows a program that calculates the average monthly temperature.

```
Line 1.    SET Total=0
Line 2.    FOR loop= 1 TO 30 DO
Line 3.            RECEIVE day_temperature FROM keyboard
Line 4.            SET Total = Total + day_temperature
Line 5.    END FOR
Line 6.    SET average=Total / 30
```

Explain what changes you would have to make to the program for months that have thirty one days.

2

Alter Line #2 from 30 to 31
Alter line 6 from 30 to 31

13. Describe the type of users who would benefit from a user interface, which had few options and large icons.

1

Users with eyesight problems

14. Explain, with reasons, what type of computer system would be most suited to travelling salesmen showing images of their latest products.

2

A tablet computer: it is light and portable, and a computer isn't necessary

MARKS | DO NOT WRITE IN THIS MARGIN

SECTION 2 — 70 marks

Attempt ALL questions

15. Alison works for a design company and has created this image using a vector graphics package.

(a) State **two** reasons why she would not have created this image using a bit-mapped graphics package.   2

Bit-mapped images take up more memory space, and cannot be easily re-sized

(b) State what standard *file type* she would use to save this file.   1

SVG

(c) Alison finds a graphic on the Internet and incorporates it into her created image to create a logo for a new bike company.   1

  (i) Explain why this is *not legal*.

  The graphic belongs to somebody else - she has broken the Copyright, Designs & Patents Act

  (ii) Explain how Alison could use the graphic *legally*.   1

  Ask permission from the owner / Buy a copy.

(d) Before Alison e-mails 200 photographs to the printing company she *compresses* the files.

  (i) Explain why the photographs require to be *compressed* before being e-mailed.   1

  The file sizes are too large for sending across the internet

  (ii) Explain what effect compression may have on the photographs.   1

  The image quality might not be as good as the original versions

Total marks   7

16. A program is used to control access to a secure area in a bank. You have **three** attempts to get the code correct before an alarm is sounded.

Here is the pseudocode for the program:

```
Line 1.        SET counter TO 1
Line 2.        REPEAT
Line 3.            RECEIVE pin FROM keypad
Line 4             IF pin<>4714 THEN
Line 5                 SEND["wrong number"] TO display
Line 6.            END IF
Line 7.            SET counter TO counter+1
Line 8.
Line 9.      IF pin=4715 THEN
Line 10.          SEND Open TO lock
Line 11.    ELSE
Line 12.          SEND Sound TO speakers
Line 13.    END IF
```

(a) Complete the missing *pseudocode* for line 8.   3

UNTIL pin=4714 OR counter=3

(b) When the program is tested with the correct code the alarm is sounded. State the *error* in the program.   1

There are two different values for the pin in the program.

(c) Explain why we need the *selection statement* after the loop has been completed.   2

There are 2 states to come out of the loop. Either the code is correct, or you have had 3 attempts and it is wrong.

(d) Why is a *conditional loop* used in the program rather than a *fixed loop*?   1

You are not sure how many times you are going to go around the loop, as you come out of it at the 1st, 2nd or 3rd attempts.

Question 16 (continued)

MARKS

DO NOT
WRITE IN
THIS
MARGIN

(e) When the computer program is written, state **two** ways in which the program can be made readable.

2

Indentation

Meaningful identifiers

(f) What *data type* is used by all the variables in the program?

1

Integer

Total marks 10

17. Below is the structured diagram for a program to automatically display the cost of posting a parcel.

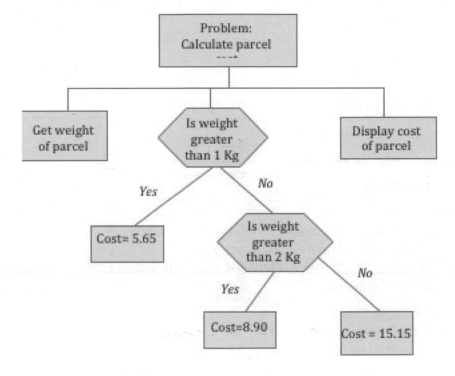

(a) Using *pseudocode*, or a programming language of your choice, write a program to implement the design above.

5

```
SET cost TO 0
RECIEVE weight FROM keyboard
IF (weight) 1 5. THEN
    SET cost to 5.65
ELSE = IF
    IF
```

Question 17 (continued)

MARKS

(b) State **four** items of data that you could use to test for extreme data, assuming that the data is entered to *two decimal places*.

2

Weight = 0.99 Kg, 0.98 Kg,
2.01 Kg, 2.02 Kg

(c) Use *pseudocode*, or a programming language of your choice, to validate the input of the weight of the parcel.

4

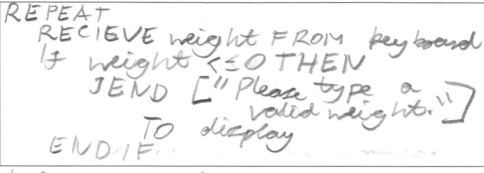

```
REPEAT
    RECIEVE weight FROM keyboard
    If weight <= 0 THEN
        SEND ["Please type a
                valid weight."]
        TO display
    ENDIF
UNTIL weight = 0
```

Total marks 11

18. Ray has received the following e-mail.

From:	dmrkenneth@rocketmail.com
Subject:	Swiss Lotto Lucky Winner
Attachments:	WinnersForm.exe
Message:	Congratulations! You have won ?750,000 pounds. To claim the prize please complete the attached text file with your name, address, age, nationality, occupation, telephone no, Bank sort code and bank account no. Mr. Kenneth Gram On-line Games Director Swiss Lotto London

(a) Explain this e-mail.

1

It is a phishing email

(b) Describe what could happen if you replied with the information that they ask for in the e-mail.

1

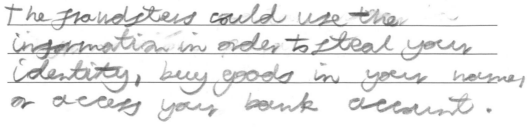

The fraudsters could use the information in order to steal your identity, buy goods in your name, or access your bank account.

Question 18 (continued)   MARKS

(c) The attached file could contain a virus.

     (i) State a reason why you could think that the attachment is a virus.   **1**

It doesn't use a standard file format for text.

     (ii) Describe **two** methods which anti-virus software use to detect viruses.   **2**

① Check it against known patterns of viruses. ② Look for suspicious activity, such as copying of address books.

(d) State which *law* you are breaking by knowingly sending viruses through e-mails.   **1**

Computer Misuse Act

                               Total marks   6

19. Charlie has a design for his web-site for his music store.

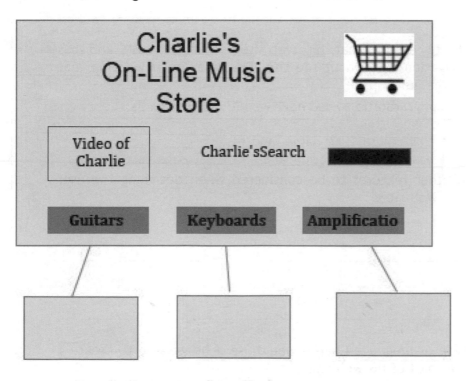

(a) What type of *links* are the Guitars, Keyboards and Amplification navigation bars?   **1**

Internal hyperlinks

Question 19 (continued)

MARKS

(b) Explain how Charlie's search engine differs from Google.   1

Internal to the website

(c) State the type of *addressing* that is used to link the home page to the instrument pages.   1

Relative referencing

(d) When Charlie tests the web-site, he finds that the video keeps *pausing*. State what you could do to the video to stop this problem occurring.   1

Reduce the sample rate

(e) Apart from testing that the video works, suggest **two** other tests that Charlie should make to ensure his web-site works correctly.   2

① Search engine works
② Shopping cart works

(f) Charlie wants to ensure that his web-site is easy to use and has consistent navigation throughout the site. Describe the *navigation* that will appear on the guitar page.   1

Some type of navigation that appears on his homepage: the three hyperlinked boxes

(g) Describe **two** other features to be considered when designing the user interface of the web-site.   2

① Layout on each screen
② Method of interaction

(h) State what type of *language* Charlie would use if he wanted to create a sign-up sheet as part of his web-site.   1

Javascript

Total marks 10

MARKS | DO NOT WRITE IN THIS MARGIN

20. Avonvalley college keep a database of their adult students and the courses they have booked.

Student no	Forename	Surname	Gender	Date of Birth	Class Code	Full Time
153889	Maureen	Bryce	Female	12/12/57	Art001	Yes
152110	Alice	Burns	Female	22/04/78	Art003	No
153227	Jasmine	Dunsmuir	Female	13/05/67	Art003	No
153647	Janice	Galloway	Female	03/06/75	Art001	Yes
153183	Bridget	Hunter	Female	07/08/55	Pho101	Yes
153856	Jan	Pavel	Male	19/07/72	Com002	No
153776	David	Perez	Male	06/02/98	Com002	No
153772	Ian	Smith	Male	01/08/58	Pho102	No

(a) Describe how the database has been sorted. 　2

Gender (Alphabetically ascending), Surname (Alphabetically ascending)

(b) The database makes use of *primary keys* and *foreign keys*.

   (i) Which field is the *primary key*? 　1

   Student No

   (ii) Explain what is meant by a "foreign key". 　1

   An attribute which appears as a primary key in another table

(c) What *field type* has been used in the Full time field? 　1

Boolean

(d) State **two** fields that can use *field range validation*. 　2

Date of birth, Class code

(e) The college uses a web-site for students to book their courses.

The students can only choose their course from a list like this:

State the type of *validation* used in this situation. 　1

Restricted choice

Question 20 (continued)   MARKS   DO NOT WRITE IN THIS MARGIN

(f) What would be the result of a search on the gender field for "female" and the Full time field for "No"?   **1**

Alice Bums, Jasmine Dunsmuir

(g) Describe **two** advantages of using an *electronic database* instead of a *manual database*.   **2**

Easier to backup
searching can be done
more quickly

Total marks 11

21. Zahera has opened up her father's laptop.

   (a) She notices that the *processor* and the *RAM* memory slots are separate.

     Describe how data is transferred from the *RAM* to the *processor*.   **1**

Along the data bus

   (b) Zahera notices that only one of the four memory slots has a *RAM chip*. Describe the benefits of adding more RAM to the laptop.   **1**

Faster performance, with memory
intensive applications, such as
video editing

   (c) The motherboard of the laptop comes with a number of types of *interface* such as the SATA interface for the hard disc drive.

     Name and describe a purpose of an *interface* that the laptop may have.   **2**

USB - attatching external
USB flash drives. Firewire -
attatching digital video
cameras

Question 21 (continued)   MARKS | DO NOT WRITE IN THIS MARGIN

(d) Zahera notices that the laptop doesn't have a *hard disc* drive but a *solid state* drive. Describe one advantage and one dis-advantage of *a solid state* drive compared to a *hard disc* drive.   **2**

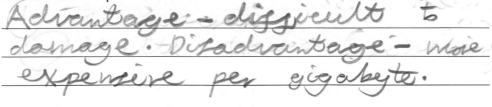

Advantage - difficult to damage. Disadvantage - more expensive per gigabyte.

(e) Zahera wants a tablet computer rather than a laptop.

Describe **two** functions of a tablet that are not always available on a laptop.   **2**

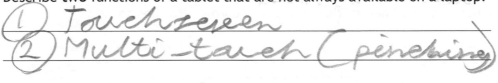

① Touchscreen
② Multi-touch (pinching)

Total marks   8

22. The following *pseudocode* has been designed to calculate the average of five test marks.

```
Line 1    RECEIVE mark1 FROM keyboard
Line 2    RECEIVE mark2 FROM keyboard
Line 3    RECEIVE mark3 FROM keyboard
Line 4    RECEIVE mark4 FROM keyboard
Line 5    RECEIVE mark5 FROM keyboard
Line 6    SET total TO mark1+mark2+mark3+mark4+mark5
Line 7    SET average TO total/5
Line 8    SEND ["The average of the five tests is ",
          average] TO DISPLAY
```

This is very inefficient code.

(a) State the most suitable *data structure* and *data type* for the variable called mark that should have been used.   **2**

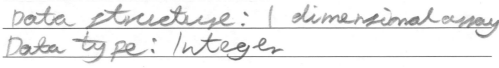

Data structure: 1 dimensional array
Data type: Integer

(b) State the most suitable *data type* for the variable called total.   **1**

Integer

Question 22 (continued)   MARKS

(c) State the type of *construct* that should have been used in line 1 to 5 to make a more efficient program.   1

Fixed loop

(d) State **two** examples of *exceptional data* that you could use to test this program.   2

-50, John o' Groates

(e) When the program is tested with *exceptional data* the programmer discovers there is a flaw to his program. What *standard algorithm* requires to be added to the program to correct this design flaw?   1

Input validation

Total marks   7

[END OF PRACTICE QUESTION PAPER]

2013 Model Paper 3

National Qualifications MODEL PAPER 3

Computing Science

Duration — 1 hour and 30 minutes

Total marks — 90

SECTION 1 — 20 marks

Attempt ALL questions in this section.

SECTION 2 — 70 marks

Attempt ALL questions in this section.

Read all questions carefully before attempting.

Write your answers in the spaces provided, using **blue** or **black** ink.

Show all workings.

HODDER
GIBSON
LEARN MORE

MARKS

SECTION 1 – 20 marks

Attempt ALL questions

1. *Repetitive Strain Injury (RSI)* is one way in which using a computer can be bad for your health. Describe one way you can prevent *RSI*.   **1**

   Take regular breaks

2. Many publications on the Internet are published as *PDF* files. What advantage do *PDF* files have over other formats?   **1**

   They can be opened by any type of computer system, without the need for

3. In order to make code readable programmers should include internal commentary in their code. Describe two other methods of making code more readable.   **2**

   Indentation
   Meaningful identifiers

4. Mary has decided to upgrade her digital camera from a *4 Megapixel* to a *12 Megapixel*. State *one* advantage and *one* disadvantage that her new photographs will have over her old photographs.   **2**

   Advantage – higher resolution, therefore better quality images.
   Disadvantage – Takes up more memory space, so will store less images on her SSD card.

5. The following code creates a random number between 1 and 100.

   ```
   Let number=INT(100*RND)+1
   ```

   RND produces a random number between 0 and 1

   INT rounds to the nearest integer

   State the type of *constructs* that RND and INT belong to.   **2**

   Pre-defined functions

MARKS | DO NOT WRITE IN THIS MARGIN

6. When Alice is buying a new computer she notices that she has *USB3* and *USB2* interfaces. Explain the advantage of *USB3* over *USB2* interfaces.   1

The data transfer rate of USB3 is much faster than USB2.

7. Many people say that the *carbon footprint* of computers is too great. Explain how computers could reduce the use of energy in other areas.   1

Home working decreases the amount of car travel.

8. A computer program is created to keep data about the temperature in towns around Scotland. The data is input through a very sensitive sensor, which gives the temperature to 5 decimal places.

    (a) What type of *program construct* would you use to ensure that the data was restricted to two decimal places?   1

    The format pre-defined function

    (b) State the *data type* that you should use to store the value of the temperature.   1

    Real

9. *ROM*, *RAM* and *Registers* all store information. Explain why *ROM* is different from *RAM* and *Registers* in the way it stores information.   1

ROM is permanent. RAM and registers are temporary, and lose all of their data when there is no power.

10. *Javascript* is used to add interactivity to web-pages and make them more dynamic.

    Describe **two** occasions when you would use *javascript* in a web-page.   2

    1) Validating data that is entered into forms
    2) Giving warnings and confirmation messages to users

11. Describe a situation when you would decide that a *flat file structure* was not appropriate for a *database* and that *linked tables* should be use.   1

When you saw that there was a great deal of data being duplicated

MARKS | DO NOT WRITE IN THIS MARGIN

12. Peter has moved into a flat and has discovered that he can access the Internet using his next-door neighbour's wi-fi. State two reasons why he has decided to get his own wired access to the Internet.

2

(1) He would be breaking the Communications Act by accessing someone else's WiFi without permission. (2) WiFi has less bandwidth than wired access, so is slower to access data.

13. State the most suitable *data structure* and *data type* required for storing 100 test marks in a computer program.

2

Data structure: 1 Dimensional array
Data type: Integer

MARKS | DO NOT WRITE IN THIS MARGIN

SECTION 2 — 70 marks

Attempt ALL questions

14. "Nile online" are designing the information form that they require their customers to complete when buying goods online.

Field Name		Field size	Field Type
Forename		25	Text
Surname		25	Text
Address		25	Text
Town		25	Text
Type of Credit card			
	Visa	1	Boolean
	Mastercard	1	Boolean
	Amex	1	Boolean
Credit Card Number		16	Numeric
Expiry Date		8	Date
Card Security Code		3	Numeric

(a) Complete the *field types* above for the information form. **2**

(b) Describe how a *presence check* could be used to validate the data. **2**

All of the fields require a presence check, except for the fact that only one is required for the "Type of Credit Card" field.

(c) State **two** fields, which could use a *length check*. **2**

Credit card number, card security code

(d) Explain which of the fields would be a suitable *primary key*. **1**

Credit card number

Total marks 7

MARKS | DO NOT WRITE IN THIS MARGIN

15. Invictus games are developing a simple paddle game for a smartphone app.

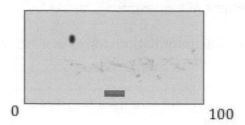

0   100

The game is to be controlled in the following manner

Press Letter Z to go left

Press letter M to move right

Press letter T to stop the game

```
Line 1     SET x=50
Line 2     REPEAT
Line 3         RECEIVE letter FROM keyboard
Line 4         IF letter="Z" AND x>0 THEN
Line 5             SET x=x-1
Line 6         END IF
Line 7
Line 8
Line 9         END IF
Line 10        SEND paddle (x,10) TO display
Line 11    UNTIL letter ="T"
```

(a) Using *pseudocode* or a language of your choice, complete the missing *pseudocode* to control the M key for line 7 and 8.   4

IF letter = "M" AND x <100 THEN
    SET x = x +1

MARKS | DO NOT WRITE IN THIS MARGIN

Question 15 (continued)

(b) Explain what happens when the program is tested with a letter other than Z, M or T.   1

Nothing happens

(c) State what *data type* is the variable called letter?   1

String

(d) Ten Points are scored if the ball touches the wall behind the paddle.

Using *pseudocode* or a language of your choice, write the line of code that increases the score.   2

*IF x = 1 THEN
SET score = score + 1*

(e) State what *hardware information* the programmers would require to ensure that their app will work on Smartphones.   1

RAM size

Total marks   9

16. The following *pseudocode* has been written to find the team with the most points.

```
Line 1    SET teams TO [Edinburgh, London, Berlin, Paris]
Line 2    SET points TO [47,27,51,51]
Line 3    SET highest TO 1
Line 4    FOR position FROM 2 TO 4
Line 5        IF points[highest]<points[position] THEN
Line 6            SET highest TO position
Line 7        END IF
Line 8    END FOR
Line 9    SEND["The winning team is "]team[highest] TO
          display
```

(a) State the *output* from the above *pseudocode*.   1

Berlin

MARKS

Question 16 (continued)

(b) Describe the *logic error* that this program has.   1

Doesn't take into account if 2 teams have the same highest score

(c) The first time the program was coded and run, line 7 had a *syntax error*. What could have been the problem?   1

A typing error, eg ENF IF

(d) State the most suitable *data structure* and *data type* for the variable team.   2

Data structure: 1 Dimensional array
Data type: string

(e) Describe what changes you would require to make to the *pseudocode* to find the team with the lowest score.   3

Change all recurrences of the variable "highest" to "lowest", change "<" to ">", change "the winning team" to "the losing team".

(f) Describe what changes you would require to make to the pseudocode if there are eight teams rather than four.   3

① Add four more team names to line 1
② Add four more points to line 2
③ Change "4" to "8" in line 4.

Total marks 11

MARKS | DO NOT WRITE IN THIS MARGIN

17. The GroundNews news agency have designed their new website.

WWW.GroundNews.org.uk	Search
UK	
Europe	
Africa	**Latest**
Asia	
America	**UFO spotted over Glasgow**

(a) What is the news agency's *URL*?   1

GroundNews.org.uk

(b) State the name of the first page of a website.   1

The home page

(c) Describe what happens when you click on the Internal *hyperlink* called Africa.   1

You are taken to a page on Africa, which is on the same site.

(d) Describe why the search page will be *limited*.   1

It's only related to this website

(e) State a suitable *standard file format* for the video clips.   1

MPEG4

(f) Comment on why this design would be suitable for use on a *smartphone*.   2

① Good visual layout
② Straight forward navigation

MARKS | DO NOT WRITE IN THIS MARGIN

Question 17 (continued)

(g) Describe **two** hardware limitations you should consider when designing web-sites for *Smartphones*.   2

① Limited RAM
② Limited processing speed.

(h) The news agency will take stories sent to them from members of the public. What must the agency do to ensure they don't break the *Copyright, Designs and Patents Act*?   1

Ensure that the stories aren't copied from other news channels

(i) Describe **three** tests that the news agency should undertake on their completed website.   3

① Search works
② Video works
③ Hyperlinks take the user to the correct pages

Total marks 13

18. The following is a price list for concerts depending on age.

• Under 18 - £5

• Between 18 and 26 - £10

• Over 27 - £20

MARKS

Question 18 (continued)

(a) Using *pseudocode* or a programming language of your choice, write a short program to output the correct ticket cost depending on the users age.   **4**

```
RECIEVE age FROM keyboard
IF age <18 THEN
    SEND ["Your ticket costs €5."]
        to display
ELSE
    IF age <27 THEN
        SEND ["Your ticket costs €10."]
            to display
    ELSE
        SEND ["Your ticket costs €20."]
            to display
    END IF
END IF
```

(b) State the *data type* that you would use for the variable age.   **1**

Integer

(c) State the *data* that you would use to check for *extreme data* in this program.   **2**

17, 18, 26, 27

(d) When the program is being developed it is run using an *interpreter*. State an advantage of using an *interpreter* rather than a *compiler* at the development of a program.   **1**

Easier to spot errors during execution

(e) When the program has completed testing a compiled version is made. State **two** advantages of a compiled version compared to an interpreted version.   **2**

① Will run faster than the interpreted version
② Doesn't need a translator

MARKS | DO NOT WRITE IN THIS MARGIN

Question 18 (continued)

(f) Explain the difference between the *high-level language code* you have created and the compiled version.   1

The compiled version is in machine code.

Total marks 11

19. Y3 are recording their latest music album using sound editing software on a laptop computer.

(a) The band want to buy an *external hard drive* to backup their songs.

State **two** criteria that they should use when deciding which external hard drive to buy.   2

① Capacity
② Data transfer speed

(b) The music files are stored in *WAV format*, which are too large to e-mail to their American producer. Explain how they could reduce the size of the files.   1

Compress to MP3

(c) Explain the advantage of saving their music files to a *cloud network*.   1

They would be able to access the files all over the world.

(d) The band are frightened that keeping their files in a *cloud network* will not be secure. Describe **two** ways in which the company running the cloud network can keep access to your files secure.   2

① Passwords
② Encryption

(e) The band have downloaded a photograph for the front cover.

Question 19 (e) (continued) MARKS

(i) Explain how the photograph is stored in the computer's *memory*. **2**

Bit - mapped, pixel by pixel

(ii) The photograph is *1200dpi* in four colours. Calculate the *storage requirements* of this graphic. Give your answer in appropriate units.

Show your working. **3**

$1200 \times 1200 \times 2 = 2,880,000$ bits

$2,880,000 / 8 = 360,000$ bytes

$360,000 / 1024 = 351.6$ KB

Total marks 11

20. Dirtcheap flights have an on-line database of all the seats that they have sold.

Surname	Initial	E-mail address	Ref No	Flight No	From	To	Date
Brown	A	rsimpson@greenet.com	43271	DH006	EDI	PRA	17015
Green	M	mgreen265@bigmail.com	43268	DH006	EDI	PRA	17015
Johns	C	cjohns@ceapnet.com	43270	DH006	EDI	PRA	17015
Khan	S	saheerakhan@bluenet.com	43269	DH006	EDI	PRA	17015
Needy	G	mgreen265@bigmail.com	43272	DH006	EDI	PRA	17015
Simpson	R	rsimpson@greenet.com	43267	DH006	EDI	PRA	17015
Taylor	R	mgreen265@bigmail.com	43273	DH006	EDI	PRA	17015
Cray	O	Crayclan@bluenet.com	43277	DH013	LHW	AMS	17015
Fallon	D	Crayclan@bluenet.com	43278	DH013	LHW	AMS	17015
Hunter	W	whunter@smalltalk.com	43274	DH013	LHW	AMS	17015
McDonald	A	andymac@bluetalk.com	43276	DH013	LHW	AMS	17015
Summer	Y	whunter@smalltalk.com	43276	DH013	LHW	AMS	17015

(a) Describe how the data has been sorted. **2**

Flight no. (Ascending), Surname (Alphabetically ascending)

MARKS

Question 20 (continued)

(b) Describe why a *relational database* is required rather than a *flat-file database*.   1

Duplication of data

(c) The database keeps crashing due to a large number of *pings* sent to the database server.

State what type of *network security* threat is being undertaken.   1

A denial of service attack

(d) Dirtcheap are criticised in the press for having a complicated *User Interface Design*. Describe **two** requirements of good interface design.   2

(1) Simple, short commands (such as Run, Insert etc)
(2) Restricted choices from pop-up menus, check boxes and radio buttons

(e) The server that runs the database has many *interfaces* for connecting to a variety of peripherals. Describe **two** reasons why *interfaces* are required.   2

(1) Peripherals run at different speeds from the processor
(2) Some peripherals are analogue, and the signals need to be converted to digital

Total marks   8

[END OF PRACTICE QUESTION PAPER]

SQA NATIONAL 5
COMPUTING SCIENCE 2013

NATIONAL 5 COMPUTING SCIENCE SPECIMEN QUESTION PAPER

Section 1

1. 00011001

2. *One of the following points needs to be given to obtain the mark.*
   - The telephone number contains a leading zero which would be dropped if stored as a number
   - The telephone number contains a space which is not valid in numeric field
   - The telephone number will not be used for calculations

3. Data Bus

4. *Examples of suitable answers are given below. The candidate must give a workstation feature and describe how it reduces a health risk.*
   One mark to be awarded for any one pair, eg:

Feature	Reason
tilt and swivel (adjustable) monitor	can be moved to the correct angle to prevent eye strain or squinting
ergonomically designed keyboard	enables user to keep hands and wrists in a natural position and avoid RSI

5. *Description should be about the purpose of JavaScript: both the following points should be made to gain the two marks. eg:*
   - JavaScript is used to add interactivity (one mark) to HTML/web pages (one mark)
   - JavaScript is used to provide dynamic content (one mark) to HTML/web pages (one mark)

6. *Candidates need to provide both parts in their answer to gain the two marks.*
   Megapixels in descending order
   Price in ascending order

7. *Candidates need to show clearly in their answer the data structure and the data type to demonstrate their understanding.*
   Data structure = Array (one mark)
   Data type = Real (one mark)

8. HTML

9. (a) *The candidate must show in their answer that they understand what is meant by a Denial of Service Attack.*
   Flooding the server with a large number of requests

   (b) *The candidate must make reference to an effect on the user.*
   It would result in the server being unavailable to its intended users

10. *The candidate needs to link their answer to security. One clear benefit would be awarded one mark, eg:*
    - Eliminate problems caused by lost IDs or forgotten passwords by using physiological attributes
    - Prevent unauthorised use of lost, stolen or "borrowed" ID cards
    - Reduce fraud by employing hard-to-forge technologies and materials
    - Replace hard-to-remember passwords which may be shared or observed

11. *Question asks about operating system design, answer needs to look at technology. (This question allows the candidate to look at operating systems in the current time so marking scheme will be relevant to the operating systems at time of marking.)*
    Any one from the following would be relevant at time of publication:
    - smartphone/tablet—operating system must have low hardware requirements
    - smartphone/tablet—operating system must deal with input from a different range of input devices
    - smartphone/tablet is a battery powered device so managing power consumption is particularly important

12. *Candidate answer could refer to either data eradication or compliance with legislation, eg:*
    Data eradication to comply with legislation such as Data Protection Act.
    Candidate should include one issue for one mark.
    - ensure data is wiped from hard disks before disposal
    - ensure personal data is not passed to future users if hard disk drive (HDD) is recycled
    - physical destruction of disks if software cannot be used to remove data

    OR:

    Compliance with legislation such as the Waste Electrical and Electronic Equipment Directive (WEEE):
    Candidate should include one issue for one mark.
    - assess the environmental impacts of computer disposal and recycling services
    - safe disposal of hazardous waste such as CRT monitors
    - recycling of circuit boards and chips to cut down carbon footprint
    - CRTs, LCD displays, printed circuit boards, batteries and flame retardant plastics are pre-treated before disposal

13. *Candidate has to show an understanding of the role of the file server with reference to the client server network—link fileserver and client server network. One mark for one point, eg:*
    - Server controls the level of access that client PCs have to shared resources
    - Server provides central storage for all network users

14. *This question required the candidate to state techniques for readability. Any two from (one mark each):*
    - Comment lines
    - Keywords capitalised
    - Code indented
    - Use meaningful variable names

15. Memory

Section 2

16. (a) *A description of any two advantages of smartphone over a desktop PC for tourists:*
    - Size/weight—smartphone fits into pocket and is easily carried on holiday
    - Internet connection using 3G—access almost anywhere—tablet might only connect using wi-fi network
    - Ability to make calls—can contact locations referred to in app using same device
    - Messaging—can book transport or tickets and get confirmation message sent directly to phone

    (b) *A description of interface feature supported by a judgement of its suitability for smart phone. Evaluations could indicate reasons why interface is suitable for smart phone.*
    - user friendliness
    - straightforward navigation
    - consistent design of elements and text
    - good visual layout

    Comments could indicate reasons why interface is not suitable for smart phone.

    (c) *Answer must name parts used to store real numbers.*
    Mantissa and exponent

    (d) (i) Answer should name any standard file format for photos such as jpeg.

    (ii) An explanation that indicates file size reduction is due to lower number of pixels that make up the image.

17. (a) (i) *Any one from:*
    Structure chart
    Flow chart

    (ii) *Should relate to answer 17(a) above.*
    A flow chart/structured chart gives a visual representation of the sequence of processes/ events.

    (b)

Variable	Data type
total	integer
distance	integer
destination	string

    (c) 12,8,6 (one mark)
    0 to finish input (one mark)

    (d) *Candidate needs to show the following statements to achieve marks. One mark for each stage.*
    IF statement
    Condition of total>50
    Suitable output message

18. (a) *A description that refers to the test being carried out on an element from the web page shown.*
    - Check Order Now button—ensure script executes correctly, and links to correct data entry form.
    - Check login button—ensure script executes correctly, data entered is validated correctly.
    - Check screen matches design—ensure correct elements on page, ensure spelling is accurate, ensure elements layout is correct.

    (b) *An explanation that indicates destination of hyperlink, supported by appropriate anchor from the web page shown.*
    Identity of internal hyperlink—in this case, link to What's On page or Performers page or Your Visit page or Box Office page.

Explanation: points to a file within a website.
Identity of external hyperlink—in this case, link to Our Sponsor's website.
Explanation: points to another website.

(c)

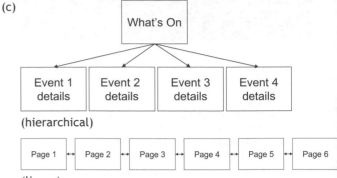

(hierarchical)

(linear)
Labelled diagram of navigation map for each page.

(d) *A description of web page feature that helps user access information such as:*
- Screen magnification/zoom feature to enlarge what is displayed on the computer monitor, making it easier to read for vision impaired users.
- Voice output option to read text on page making it easier for users with reading or learning difficulties.
- Voice output option to read out text and commands available so site can be used by blind and vision impaired users.
- Careful choice of colour scheme helps avoid problems with colour blindness and some low vision eyesight issues.
- Careful choice of font helps readability.

(e) (i) *Response should state any one of the eight principles to be met by data controllers under Data Protection Act.*
- Personal data must be processed fairly and lawfully
- Personal data must be obtained for specified and lawful purposes
- Personal data must be adequate, relevant and not excessive
- Personal data must be accurate and up to date
- Personal data must not be kept any longer than necessary
- Personal data must be processed in accordance with the data subject's rights
- Personal data must be kept securely
- Personal data must not be transferred to any other country without adequate protection in situ

(ii) *An explanation that includes why the principle stated in 18e(i) is important to customers.*
Customers are concerned about the amount of data stored, about how the data is used and how long it is kept. Compliance with DPA reassures customers that companies are handling their data in an appropriate manner, taking precautions against threats against computer security and ensuring data is correct.
- Personal data must be processed fairly and lawfully.
- Customers will not be deceived or misled as to why the information is needed and will have to give their permission for data to be stored.
- Personal data must be obtained for specified and lawful purposes.

- Customers know what their data is being used for and that it cannot be used for any other unrelated purpose, or that their data cannot be given away or sold without them knowing.
- Personal data must be adequate, relevant and not excessive.
- Customers will be able to know exactly what data items are kept about them and the reason they are kept so that they do not need to divulge other personal information.
- Personal data must be accurate and up to date.
- Customers know that inaccurate, incorrect, or out-of-date data will not be used by the company.
- Personal data must not be kept any longer than necessary.
- Customers know that their data will be destroyed after a certain period of time.
- Personal data is processed in accordance with the data subject's rights.
- Customers know that they have the right to see their own data, check its accuracy, prevent processing that may cause harm/distress, and can claim compensation for any damage caused by breach of legislation.
- Personal data must be kept securely.
- Customers are assured that their data is only accessible to those with permission to process it, and not accessible to anyone else.
- Personal data must not be transferred to any other country without adequate protection in situ.
- Customers know their data cannot be passed outside the EU unless the country that the data is being sent to has a suitable data protection law.

19. (a) Interface

(b) *Candidate needs to state clearly what happens on each of line 3 and line 7 for one mark each.*
Line 3, OR should be AND
Line 7, speed_of_car = 100 should be speed_of_car = 0

(c) (i)

Test data	Type of test data
car speed – 30 mph, distance – 15 m	**extreme**
car speed – 14 mph, distance – 8 m	normal
car speed – 45 mph, distance – 17 m	normal
car speed – "Bernard", distance – "-12 m"	exceptional

(ii) To ensure that the program can cope with a variety of input without crashing.

20. (a) *A description that indicates reason for linking tables with reference to data in the question.*
Any one from:
- Less data duplication with linked tables — details of instructor will only be entered once.
- Less inconsistency in data due to less duplication – as name of instructor only entered once, then only one version exists.
- Better data integrity.
- Removes multi-value fields — more than one set of course details for an instructor so they should be moved to separate table.

- Easier to search single value fields — without linking tables course detail field will contain several values which make searching difficult.

(b) (i) A named field is identified as the primary key for each table.
Primary Keys
INSTRUCTOR   Instructor ID (one mark)
COURSE   Course Reference (one mark)

(ii) *An explanation that covers why foreign key is necessary.*
To enable tables to be linked—foreign key is the primary key in other table.

(c) *Response must name two data types that are suitable for the data in the scenario.*
Any two from:
Text
Date
Graphic (or object)

(d) *Candidate must specify the correct type of validation check using appropriate terminology and provide details of how it is used in this example.*
Type of validation: Restricted choice
Description of use: Limits values that can be entered to a list of acceptable value (days of week)

(e) Candidate must identify two features in the email and give a reason why each might be suspicious.
- Subject "Please update account" – not usual for company to ask this
- Dear Customer—registered customer would be addressed by specific reference not generic term
- Click the link—URL stated in link is different to actual URL transferred to
- Incorrect use of spelling and grammar—not used by professional business

(f) *An explanation that demonstrates understanding of the security risks if the link is clicked.*
Any two from:
- Phishing email
- Attempt by hackers to gain personal login details to access bank account
- Redirect to unofficial site where customer enters details and sends them directly to hacker
- Hacking of account details may lead to online fraud or identity theft

21. (a)

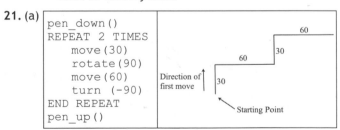

```
pen_down()
REPEAT 2 TIMES
    move(30)
    rotate(90)
    move(60)
    turn (-90)
END REPEAT
pen_up()
```

Staircase shape with four lines
Correct distances of 30 and 60 noted
Starting point

(b) Fixed loop
Explanation of program loops a fixed number of times

(c) 600 x 600 bytes (8 bits per pixel)
360000/1024 kilobytes
351.6 kilobytes

22. (a) (i) IF length of textfield7 >=8 THEN
               SET valid TO true
            END IF
            Alternative answers are possible. Marks to be
            awarded for correct use of IF, correct use of
            condition involving textfield7 and a correct action
            as a result eg setting a flag variable.

    (ii) *A description that covers the following points:*
         Values entered on form for "Create a password"
         and "Confirm your password" assigned to
         variables
         If statement used to compare these variables
         If the values match then a screen is shown
         confirming registration, otherwise an error
         message is displayed.

    (b) *A description that covers two reasons why cloud
        storage is better than USB storage.*
        Cloud storage is less vulnerable to loss, damage or
        theft than USB flash drive
        Cloud storage scalable to requirements rather than
        fixed capacity of a USB flash drive
        Cloud storage solutions include automatic backup of
        data whereas you need to set up a backup routine
        yourself with a USB flash drive

23. (a) For days 1-7
               let total= total+bpm (days)
            next days
            let average bpm=total/7

    (b) *Clear description must identify the following for all
        three marks:*
        • Implementation of conditional loop and the fact
          that condition is NOT met as number entered
          negative.
        • Input value from keyboard.
        • If statement with condition being met as data
          entered is negative, a negative error message is
          displayed and user asked to re-enter (one mark).

    (c) (i) Machine code

        (ii) *Any two from:*
             Creates standalone executable code
             Code will execute faster
             Can create portable code

NATIONAL 5 COMPUTING SCIENCE MODEL PAPER 1

Section 1

1.	Binary	1
2.	33	1
3.	Buses	1
4.	Save them as a standard file format such as RTF.	1
5.	Not as expensive and not such a high storage capacity.	2
6.	Can be accessed from anywhere in the world.	1
7.	Encrypted	1
8.	Copyright, Designs & Patents Act	1

9. Pseudocode
   flow chart
   structured diagram   1

10. The first things you type are your user ID and password
    (1 mark)
        which would then be accessible to the owner of the
    keylogging software. (1 mark)   2

11. RAM size
    Processor Speed
    Storage capacity
    One mark for each valid point with a maximum of 2.   2

12.	OR should be an AND	1
13.	No meaningful identifiers	1
14.	Web creation	1
15.	Moving to another webpage	1
16.	Conditional loop	1
17.	Syntax Error	1

Section 2

18. (a) Portable
        Smaller footprint   2

    (b) No security
        Difficult to create a methodical backup regime   2

    (c) Description of:
        • Retina scanning (1 mark)
        • Finger prints (1 mark)   2

    (d) Ensure data is wiped from the hard-disc drives
        Physical destruction of hard discs if software cannot
        be used to remove data   1

    (e) Ensure that the equipment is re-cycled or re-used.
        (1 mark)
        The metals inside should be safely extracted. (1
        mark)   2

19. (a) Height>200 (1 mark) OR (1 mark) weight>2.4 (1 mark) 3

    (b)

Type of test data	Test Data	
Normal	Height – 100	,weight – 2.2
Extreme	Height – 200	,weight – 2.4
Exceptional	Height – 250	,weight – 2.5

                                                               3

    (c) As it should be impossible to have a weight or height
        below zero the program should ask for a positive value. 1

    (d) A wireless connection   1

20. (a)
```
REPEAT 4 TIMES
    Forward(100)
    Right(90)
END REPEAT
Right(135)
Move(50)
Left(135)
REPEAT 4 TIMES
    Forward(100)
    Right(90)
END REPEAT
```
    3

   (b) • Less memory required
       • Can be re-sized
       • Not-resolution dependant
       One mark for each valid point with a maximum of 2. **2**

   (c) 400x400x2=320000
       320000/8 = 40000 bits
       40000/1024 = 39.0625 Kilobytes   **3**

   (d) BMP
       JPEG   **1**

21. (a) Using small rather than capital letters
       finding the correct letter on the keyboard   **2**

   (b)
```
RECEIVE answer FROM keyboard (1 mark)
WHILE answer<>A,B,C or D (1 mark)
    DISPLAY ["Invalid Input, try again"] (1 mark)
    RECEIVE answer FROM keyboard (1 mark)
END WHILE
```
    4

   (c) Initialise the variable wrong and right to the values 0
       (1 mark)
       If the answered received from the keyboard is equal
       to C
       Then add 1 to the correct variable (1 mark)
       If the answer is not equal to C then add 1 to the
       wrong variable (1 mark)   **3**

   (d) Shows errors   **1**

22. (a) Line 2 - Value of temperature is 16.3
       Line 3 - Checks if temperature is less than 10 –
       No so goes to line 5
       Line 6 - Checks if temperature is greater than 20 –
       No so goes to line 8
       Line 9 – goes back to line 1 unless switch is off   **4**

   (b) Mantissa and exponent   **2**

   (c) Boolean   **1**

   (d) Interfaces   **1**

   (e) Internal Commentary   **1**

23. (a) Boolean   **1**

   (b) Hyperlink   **1**

   (c) To uniquely identify each record   **1**

   (d) Register with the office of the Information
       Commissioner   **1**

   (e) Search on the field New Cd = Yes (1mark) AND (1
       mark) field Town="Dundee" (1 mark)   **3**

   (f) • Data duplication
       • Data inconsistency or update/deletion/insertion
         anomalies
       • Data integrity errors (due to data inconsistency)
       • Inconsistent search results in multi-value fields
         Any one for 1 mark   **1**

   (g) None as an address could be any combination of text.   **1**

24. (a) No return to home page buttons on the web-pages   **1**

   (b) Hyperlinks   **1**

   (c) Links work
       Checkout works   **2**

   (d) www.SCOTXCLOTHES.co.uk   **2**

   (e) Encryption   **1**

   (f) • Appropriate tags   **1**
       • buy a sponsored link   **1**

   (g) Scripting language   **1**

25. (a) In case it has been used as a variable previously and
       already contains a value.   **1**

   (b) Fixed   **1**

   (c) Arithmetic expression   **1**

   (d) Total – Integer
       Day – string
       average – real   **3**

   (e) One dimensional array   **1**

NATIONAL 5 COMPUTING SCIENCE MODEL PAPER 2

Section 1

1. MP3 has had some data removed while WAV has had no data removed.   1

2. Syntax   1

3. Mantissa and exponent   2

4. The bold tag has not been closed.   1

5. The address bus   1

6. To store text   1

7. To convert high level language into machine code so that it can be understood by the computer   1

8. Decrease resolution   1

9. (a) Communications Act   1

    (b) Passwords   1

10. No additional hardware or software required.   1

11. Search on the field Town=Inverness(1 mark) AND (1 mark) Date of birth<1/1/1996 (1 mark)   3

12. Alter line 2 from 30 to 31
Alter line 6 from 30 to 31   2

13. Small children or users with eyesight problems   1

14. Tablet, as it is light and portable and a keyboard isn't necessary.   2

Section 2

15. (a) It takes up less memory
Can easily re-size objects   2

    (b) SVG   1

    (c) (i) The graphic belongs to someone else – she has broken the Copyright Designs and Patents ACT.   1

       (ii) Ask permission from the owner or buy a copy.   1

    (d) (i) The file sizes are too large for sending across the Internet   1

       (ii) The quality might not be as good as the original   1

16. (a) UNTIL Pin=4714(1 mark) OR (1 mark) counter=3 (1 mark)   3

    (b) There are two different values for the pin in the program.   1

    (c) There are two states to come out of the loop. Either the code is correct or you have had 3 attempts and the code is wrong.   2

    (d) You are not sure how many times you are going to go around the loop as you could come out of the loop at the first, second or third attempt.   1

    (e) Indentation
meaningful identifiers   2

    (f) Integers   1

17. (a) SET cost TO 0
RECEIVE weight FROM keyboard (1 mark)
IF weight<1 THEN
    SET cost TO 5.65(1 mark)
ELSE
    IF weight<2 THEN(1 mark)
       SET cost TO 8.90
    ELSE

       SET cost TO 15.15(1 mark)
    END IF
END IF
SEND["cost of parcel is]cost TO display(1 mark)   5

    (b) 0.9, 1.0 ,1.9 ,2.0   2

    (c) REPEAT (1 mark)
    RECEIVE weight FROM keyboard (1 mark)
    IF weight<=0 THEN(1 mark)
       SEND[type a valid weight] TO display(1 mark)
    END IF
UNTIL weight<=0   4

18. (a) It is a Phishing e-mail.   1

    (b) The fraudsters could use the information to steal your identity, buy goods in your name or access your bank accounts.   1

    (c) (i) Doesn't use a standard file format for text   1

       (ii) Checks it against known binary patterns of viruses Looks for suspicious activity, such as copying of address books   2

    (d) The Computer Misuse Act.   1

19. (a) Internal hyperlink   1

    (b) Internal to the web-site   1

    (c) Relative referencing   1

    (d) Reduce the sample rate   1

    (e) Search engine works, navigation bars go to correct pages, shopping cart works   2

    (f) Same type of navigation bar that appears on his homepage, the three red hyperlinked boxes   1

    (g) Layout on each screen/screen design, method of interaction, choice of font/size/styles, accessible to all users   2

    (h) Javascript   1

20. (a) 'Gender' field into ascending order and 'surname' (or clas code) field into ascending order   2

    (b) (i) Student no   1

       (ii) Foreign key is an attribute which appears in another table as a primary key   1

    (c) Text   1

    (d) Student no, date of birth and class code   2

    (e) Restricted choice   1

    (f) Alice Burns and Jasmine Dunsmuir   1

    (g) Searching / sorting can be done very quickly/more easily
Data can be updated very quickly/more easily
Data analysis and reporting can be done very easily
Searches and sorts are done accurately
Easier to backup
Less space taken up   2

21. (a) Along the data bus   1

    (b) Faster performance with memory intensive applications such as video editing   1

    (c) USB – attaching external Flash drives
Firewire – attaching digital video cameras   2

    (d) Advantage – difficult to damage
Disadvantage – more expensive per gigabyte, not available in the all capacities   2

    (e) Touchscreen, multi-touch (pinching)   2

22. (a) One dimensional integer array   2

    (b) Real   1

    (c) Fixed loop   1

    (d) A negative number, text   2

    (e) Input validation   1

NATIONAL 5 COMPUTING SCIENCE MODEL PAPER 3

Section 1

1. • Adjust your chair and desk so that you are sitting without straining
   • Use alternative mice or keyboards
   • Take regular breaks
   • Use speech recognition software   1

2. Can be opened by any type of computer system without the need for specific applications or operating system software.   1

3. Indentation (1 mark)
   Meaningful variable names (1 mark)   2

4. Advantage – Higher resolution therefore better quality images. (1 mark)
   Disadvantage – Takes up much more memory than previously so will store less images on her SSD card. (1 mark)   2

5. Pre-defined (1 mark) functions (1 mark)   2

6. The Data Transfer rate of USB3 is much faster than USB2.   1

7. • Home working decreases the amount of car travel.
   • Video conferencing reduces the amount of flights taken by business people.   1

8. (a) A pre-defined function e.g. INT or Round   1
   (b) Real   1

9. ROM is permanent. RAM and Registers are temporary and lose all the data when there is no power.   1

10. Validate data that is entered into forms
    Give warnings and confirmation messages to users
    Add check buttons, radio buttons and command buttons
    Provide information on the system date and time.
    (Any two from the above list)   2

11. When you saw that there was a great deal of data being duplicated.   1

12. He was committing a crime through the Communications Act by accessing someone else Wi-Fi without permission (1 mark)
    Wi-Fi has less bandwidth than wired access and so is slower to access data (1 mark)   2

13. Structure – One dimensional array (1 mark)
    Data Type – integer (1 mark)   2

Section 2

14. (a)

Field Name	Field size	Field Type
Forename	25	*Text*
Surname	25	*Text*
Address	25	*Text*
Town	25	*Text*
Type of Credit card		
Visa	1	*Boolean*
Mastercard	1	*Boolean*
Amex	1	*Boolean*
Credit Card Number	16	*Numeric*
Expiry Date	8	*Date*
Card Security Code	3	*Numeric*

2

(b) All the fields require a presence check except only one required in type of credit card   2

(c) Credit card no, expiry date, Card security code.   2

(d) Credit card Number   1

15. (a) IF letter="M" (1 mark) AND (1 mark) x<100 THEN (1 mark)
SET x=x+1 (1 mark)   4

(b) Nothing happens   1

(c) string   1

(d) SET score TO (1 mark) score +10 (1 mark)   2

(e) Amount of RAM   1

16. (a) Berlin   1

(b) doesn't take into account if two teams have the same highest score   1

(c) A typing error e.g. ENF IF   1

(d) one dimensional string array   2

(e) Change variable highest to lowest (1 mark)
change < to > (1 mark)
change "the winning team" to the "losing team" (1 mark)   3

(f) Add four more team names to Line 1
Add four more points to line 2
Change 4 to 8 in line 4   3

17. (a) GroundNews.org.uk   1

(b) Home page   1

(c) You are taken to a page on Africa on the site   1

(d) It's only related to this web-site   1

(e) MPEG4   1

(f) Limited controls
Straight forward navigation
Good visual layout   2

(g) Limited RAM
Limited processing speed   2

(h) Ensure that the stories aren't copied from other news channels.   1

(i) Hyperlinks take them to the correct pages
Search works
Video works   3

18. (a) Line 1   RECEIVE age FROM keyboard (1 mark)
Line 2   IF age<18 THEN (1 mark)
Line 3   SEND["Your ticket cost £ 5"] TO DISPLAY
Line 4   ELSE
Line 5   IF age<27 THEN (1 mark)
Line 6   SEND["Your ticket cost £ 10"] TO DISPLAY
Line 7   ELSE   (1 mark)
Line 8   SEND["Your ticket cost £ 20"] TO DISPLAY
Line 9   END IF
Line 10   END IF   4

(b) Integer   1

(c) 17, 18, 26, 27   2

(d) Easier to spot errors during execution   1

(e) Will run faster than interpreted version.
Doesn't need translator.   2

(f) The compiled version is in machine code.   1

19. (a) Capacity and data transfer speed.   2

(b) Compress to MP3   1

(c) Could access the files from anywhere in the world.   1

(d) Passwords, Encryption   2

(e) (i) Bit-mapped pixel by picxel   2
   (ii) 1200 x 1200 x 2 = 2880000 bits (1 mark)
      2880000 / 8 = 360000 bytes (1 mark)
      360000 / 1024 = 351.6 Kb (1 mark)   3

20. (a) Flight number then surname   2

(b) Duplication of data   1

(c) Denial of Service Attack.   1

(d) Simple short commands such as Run, Insert etc (1 mark)
Restricted choices from pop-up menus, check boxes and radio buttons. (1 mark)   2

(e) Peripherals run at different speeds from the processor
Some peripherals are analogue and the signals need to be converted to digital   2

Acknowledgements

Hodder Gibson would like to thank the SQA for use of any past exam questions that may have been used in model papers, whether amended or in original form.